In his book, *Return to the Margins*, Dr. Terry Coy sounds a sobering but hopeful call to faithfulness to the Gospel in our rapidly changing world. He reminds us in a sweeping review of church history that the church has always been at its best when it had the least in terms of worldly power, popularity, and prosperity. Leaders need this helpful resource to prepare the church for the new terrain we will have to navigate in the days to come.

Dr. Michael D. Dean
Senior Pastor
Travis Avenue Baptist Church
Fort Worth, Texas

Underneath the noses of evangelicals, the continuing secularization of America has made the population within her borders the third largest mission field in the world. After his landmark book *Facing the Change*, Dr. Coy gives us a powerful reminder of how we can evangelize America from where we began: a marginalized segment of the population. This book will challenge every evangelical Christian to embrace the marginalization (and persecution) by forging ahead with the proclamation of the gospel to every segment of American society.

Aaron Meraz, PhD, DMin
W. A. Criswell Chair of Evangelism
Assistant Professor of Church Planting & Revitalization
Director of the Church Planting and Revitalization Center at Criswell College

How will Christians live in the post-Christendom era? Terry Coy provides an excellent answer to this question in this, his second book. Christians must learn to engage the culture from the margins, just as Jesus did! This means we learn to give up our attitude of religious privilege and societal dominance and rely totally upon the gospel itself, which is the way Jesus always intended. Coy explains how Christendom has collapsed in American culture and provides an excellent equipping guide to show Christians how to live in this new world.

Page Brooks, PhD
Assistant Professor of Theology and Culture
New Orleans Baptist Theological Seminary

Terry Coy addresses the questions we ▨▨▨▨ ▨▨▨▨ ▨
experiences a cultural shift. The rea▨▨▨ ▨▨▨▨▨▨▨▨▨
us to retreat but to live in such ▨▨▨▨▨▨▨ ▨▨▨▨▨▨▨▨it-
ing for the church to the margin▨▨▨▨ ▨▨▨▨▨ for His
glory. As the church we must res▨▨▨▨ ▨▨▨aith, biblical
lifestyle, and courage. Terry breath▨▨▨ ▨▨ical strategy into
our hearts. This is a must read for a▨ ▨▨▨ Jesus and His church.

Pastor Scott Weatherford
Vaughn Forest Church
Montgomery, Alabama

Return to the Margins is a great marriage of historical perspective and helpful prescription. Dr. Coy does a thorough job of recounting the place of Christianity in society: beginning at the margins of society, moving to the center of society, and now back to the margins. This recounting should challenge the church to redefine itself with the hope that revival will come. Dr. Coy does well to make a diagnosis AND offer a helpful prescription.

David Smith
Executive Director
Austin Baptist Association
Austin, Texas

Although Terry does not hold to my view that the Founding Fathers overwhelmingly embraced orthodox Christianity, we are in full agreement with his basic premise that true Christianity is at its best when we are in the margins of society. Since we find ourselves in the margins politically, culturally, and even religiously in this great nation that has turned away from God, Terry's insights are particularly relevant. *Return to the Margins* will undoubtedly become required reading in many Christian Colleges and Universities, Bible study curriculum for churches and Bible studies, as well as an important resource for Christians to have on their bookshelves at home. My prayer is that this book will be the spark that ignites the fire of revival in the true church in the United States of America and around the world.

Jeff Nyberg, PhD
Pastor, Stepping Stones Church
Executive Director
Stepping Stones Church Planting Ministry, McKinney, Texas

In *Return to the Margins* Terry Coy draws from his work in church history, missions, and theology to both describe the present position of the American church as well as chart a path forward. Rather than lament the current situation, Coy claims that working from the margins better enables the church to declare the true gospel. This book is of great benefit to church leaders who are struggling to understand the times and uncertain about how to move forward.

E. Randall Adams, PhD
Executive Director-Treasurer
Northwest Baptist Convention

Return to the Margins

Return to the Margins

Understanding and Adapting as a Church to Post-Christian America

Terry Coy

ANEKO Press

Cover Design: Amber Burger

Editors: Sheila Wilkinson, Nancy L. Graves

Printed in the United States of America

www.lifesentencepublishing.com

LIFE SENTENCE Publishing books are available at discounted prices for ministries and other outreach.

Find out more by contacting us at info@lspbooks.com

ANEKO Press, LIFE SENTENCE Publishing, and its logo are trademarks of LIFE SENTENCE Publishing, LLC

P.O. Box 652

Abbotsford, WI 54405

RELIGION / Christian Church / General

Paperback ISBN: 978-1-62245-229-3

Ebook ISBN: 978-1-62245-230-9

10 9 8 7 6 5 4 3 2 1

This book is available from www.amazon.com, Barnes & Noble, and your local bookstore.

Share this book on Facebook:

Dedicated to persecuted brothers and sisters in Christ all around the world. May your commitment, obedience, and faithfulness be eternally rewarded and convict those of us basking in our comfort.

Contents

Foreword

Opportunity at the margins

I love sharing the stories of how our missionaries are introducing people to Christ even in the most difficult of situations. I had an opportunity to do that when I introduced David Pothier, one of our church planting missionaries serving in Montreal, to a large group of pastors and others.

David was born and raised in Québec. It is probably the place in North America with the fewest evangelical Christians as a percentage of the population. Less than 1 percent of David's fellow Québécois are evangelical believers. The great hesitance about Christianity is due to a backlash against the Catholic Church that took place decades ago.

For quite some time, Montreal has been a graveyard for new churches. It is a very difficult place to start and sustain an ongoing ministry. Still, David felt a strong urging from God to be part of starting a new church in Montreal to reach the city's residents for Christ. So on April 7, 2013, he launched La Chapelle.

In such an environment, seeing fifty or sixty people become regular attenders would have been very encouraging. But today, David's church is averaging more than 700 each week! That would be an amazing thing even in the heart of the Bible belt. But it is nothing short of a miracle for Montreal.

I asked David what the secret was for drawing such a large

crowd in a city so hardened toward Christianity. Was it an effective direct mail campaign? Billboard advertising? Door-to-door outreach? Maybe social media?

His answer was pretty amazing, but shouldn't have been surprising. He said La Chapelle's numbers have grown because the believers who are attending the church are inviting their lost friends. A core group preparing to launch the church in its early days began talking to their friends and new people they met about the church and what God was doing in their lives. Many of those people decided to check out the church for themselves. Some of them gave their lives to Christ and started talking to their friends about what God was doing in them and how much they enjoyed the church.

If you're familiar with Acts 2:42-47, this might sound a little familiar. As the New Testament church allowed God's Word and the Holy Spirit to transform their lives, they loved each other, served each other and sacrificed for each other. They formed a community that helped them persevere in the face of persecution and tough times. They weren't just showing up for Sunday morning worship and racing out of the parking lot as fast as they could to get the best table at Cracker Barrel – these people were living life together in Christ!

What God has done at La Chapelle in Montreal proves that this model for how The Church is supposed to look and behave is still a very compelling attraction for people. Even among people who have grown up in a secular culture. Even among people who don't know Scripture. Even in a society that is suspicious of Christianity.

David's church is not the only one gaining traction in Montreal. Several of our church planting missionaries are building strong congregations.

We can all learn some lessons from La Chapelle as our

world grows increasingly indifferent or even callous toward Christianity.

First, we must *live missionally*. That requires intentional efforts to connect with people who don't know Christ and to communicate with them about spiritual things. Our motivation is not simply to add to our numbers at church but to introduce them to the God who loves them and created them. For some of us, that might mean becoming more familiar with Scripture or learning some techniques for turning conversations toward God and the gospel. We must be intentional in this area of life.

Next, we must *live relationally*. If anyone out there still thinks that a "If we build it, they will come" approach to church will work, it's time to abandon that illusion once and for all. People are growing tired and less responsive to the traditional ways we have promoted our churches and our faith. But over and over again, our research shows that people still respond to personal invitations. Get to know people. Show them you care. Be their friend and then an invitation to church or a conversation about faith will be more natural.

Third, we must *live faithfully*. Our society views almost everything with a certain amount of suspicion. That is why our faith – as churches and individuals – must be lived out authentically. People know you are not perfect, so admit it. As you live out your faith with authenticity, they will grow to respect you for what you believe. Demonstrate your faith in tangible ways. Show how Christianity compels us to care for people and serve people. Many of those who skip church every Sunday are serving your community. What would compel them to check out your faith if they don't see a compassionate side that is impacting people where you live and beyond.

As we live our lives in this way, there are no areas in which Christians should not have a presence. Our government, educational system, entertainment, business – all are mission fields to which we are called. And if we are living life like the believers in Acts chapter 2, we will see the power of Christ changing lives around us, and His church will grow.

Like David, Terry Coy illustrates from history how the church began at the margins, moved to the center, and now returns to the margins. In *Return to the Margins, he* describes the reasons for this return and how disciples of the church can benefit and grow as individuals and together while bringing the gospel to the people in their individual circles.

Kevin Ezell
President
North American Mission Board, SBC

Acknowledgments

Many thanks are due to several people. For one, thanks (once again) to Dr. Robby Partain, Director of Missions of Bluebonnet Baptist Association in New Braunfels, Texas. Besides being a good friend, Robby is an honest and helpful reader. He asked probing questions, pointed out needed corrections, and made significant suggestions as he read each chapter.

Thanks also to Kenneth Priest, Director of Convention Strategies for the Southern Baptists of Texas Convention. I, and others, lean on his experience and expertise in publishing in order to do things well and as quickly as possible.

Thanks to my other reader, my Dad. His constant encouragement and compliments through the writing process meant a lot.

Finally, thanks to my sweet Sandy for always believing in me, encouraging me, and letting me spend so much time researching and writing.

Introduction

In my book, *Facing the Change: Challenges and Opportunities for an American Missiology*, I argued that cultural and demographic changes in the United States mean we are living in a diverse and complex mission field. The only way for the evangelical church to reach the American mission field is to address and clarify significant Christological confusion, re-examine the nature and character of America herself, and to contextualize the unchanging message of the gospel for a rapidly changing country. Although this contextual mission, carried out with both boldness and humility, is our aim in the twenty-first century, we must be prepared to undertake the mission from a *new* place and a *new* status. We must be prepared to move, to adjust, to the already current trend – from the center of society to the margins.

Perhaps "new" is not the correct term. My premise for this book is that American evangelicals must prepare themselves, once again, for life at the margins of society. We must be prepared for a significant loss of the traditional and expected status, respect, influence, and even power we have enjoyed at the center of society during the civil religion days of our American history, and particularly, during the Moral Majority and Christian Right days of the last half-century (this is not really news to anyone paying attention). Being at the center meant we could make certain assumptions about biblical literacy, moral and ethical behavior, child rearing and marriage, education, and even politics. We could pray openly, evoking the name of Jesus. We could assume most people attended church, had grown up in church, or at least had some understanding of what church was about. We did not hesitate to refer to America as a "Christian" nation. Now, whether or not these assumptions were valid, true, or even desirable, we hesitate to make them, except, perhaps, in some areas deep in the Bible Belt – and maybe not even there anymore. Goodbye center, hello margins.

To repeat myself, this return to the margins is not a new status. I will argue it has been the predominant and even most beneficial status of biblical Christianity in history, and currently is throughout the world today. The margins of society have historically been where the church has lived most fruitfully, where spiritual pruning takes place, and where spiritual awakening and church revival often begins. Biblically, the margins of society were where Jesus lived and usually ministered, and where the early church blossomed. The margins, therefore, although frightening in their implications, are also exciting because of the new opportunities and paradigms they present for theology, mission, and ministry.

But, first, who and what are these evangelicals who are forced to the margins? Am I predicting a total loss of Christian influence and a marginalization of every branch and every aspect of Christianity? Not yet. A return to the margins does not mean total persecution, oppression, or elimination of all Judeo-Christian influence. It does mean, however, a significant reduction of that influence. A return to the margins does not mean that all versions of Christianity will find themselves marginalized. To the contrary, when I refer to *evangelicals* or the *evangelical church*, I am speaking of those Christians who hold to the historical orthodox doctrines of the faith that include the authority, veracity, and inspiration of Scripture. They espouse the exclusivity of Jesus Christ, salvation by grace alone through faith alone, the necessity of personal conversion, the reality of heaven and hell, and a belief in fulfilling the Great Commission, both personally and corporately. This definition transcends numerous denominations and religious groupings, including most adherents of some denominations and perhaps fewer in others.[1]

The cultural, political, and moral issues, however, are a bit more complicated. There are particular moral understandings and applications of Scripture shared by non-evangelical groups (many Roman Catholics in particular) that will also push them to the margins. Specifically, the biblical definition of marriage as between one man and one woman, the view that homosexual behavior is sin, and the sanctity of all human life, including that of the unborn, are beliefs which continue to be seen at best as intolerant, "fundamentalist," and hateful even among some main line Protestant groups. There are, and will continue to be, many denominations, churches, and self-described Christians who do not agree with my definition of evangelical, my explanation of biblical Christianity, and much less with my convictions (dogmatism?) on marriage and abortion. My purpose is not to pass judgment on their individual salvation, spirituality, or relationship with God. Instead, my purpose is to show that Christians who *do* believe and hold to these moral and theological positions will be pushed further and further to the margins of our secular society.

But what are the margins? What I mean by the margins will be further developed throughout this book. Suffice it to say here that the margins imply:

---

1   Numerous qualifiers and variables could be attached to this definition, including eschatological positions, church-state relationship, understanding of baptism, ministry priorities, social justice issues, and so on. These are important issues; however, I am seeking the best irreducible minimums possible for my working definition. For a comprehensive discussion of what it means to be an evangelical, see "An Evangelical Manifesto: A Declaration of Evangelical Identity and Public Commitment," May 7, 2008: Washington, D.C. Copyright by the Evangelical Manifesto Steering Committee.

1. Loss of freedom to articulate and express these beliefs, particularly in the academic world, in the political arena, and in the media. There will be greater restrictions on "hate speech," which will include preaching and teaching the exclusivity of Jesus Christ, that homosexual behavior is sin, and even the overt practice of evangelism.

2. The potential loss of educational and job opportunities, career advancement, and business freedom due to these beliefs.

3. A subsequent loss of influence in schools, government, and society in general.

4. The possible loss of tax-exempt status for churches and religious organizations and increased restrictions on the purchase of property and buildings.

5. An ever increasing perception of evangelicals as intolerant, divisive, and backward.

But, one may ask, "Aren't most of these restrictions unconstitutional?" They certainly are, but it won't matter. What is guaranteed in the Constitution and what society practices are often two different things. We need to insist on their unconstitutionality, but witness, for example, the slow evolution of women's suffrage and civil rights. In fact, that is just the argument from the gay rights movement: to restrict gay marriage is unconstitutional. My point is that being forced to the margins does not require anything as radical as a constitutional change. All that is required is a change in how the Constitution is understood and applied, and a gradual change in cultural worldview and societal practice. The bottom line is that *we* evangelicals will be considered the intolerant and unconstitutional ones. Therefore, back to the margins.

In Part One of this book, I examine the reasons for the return to the margins, which include the collapse of Christendom, the fading of American civil religion, and the apparent triumph of secularization.

Part Two deals with preparing for the return. The underlying issue in this historical movement is the issue of authority. The question evangelicals (every person really) will have to answer is, who and what is our authority? Additionally, in order to get ready for the inevitable move to the margins, what can we learn from history and from our brethren around the globe? Finally, what must change in our hearts and minds?

Part Three briefly evaluates the return, listing specific reasons to fear the return, reasons to rejoice in the return, and reasons to trust in the midst of the return. In the end, whether or not my analysis is even close to accurate, we must remember that God is sovereign and he is on a mission, that we are his instruments in that mission to redeem all of creation, and he will not fail.

Questions for Reflection and Discussion

1. How do you define an evangelical?

2. Is the author's premise that "American evangelicals must prepare themselves, once again, for life at the margins of society" realistic, or is he overstating the case? Why?

3. On page three is a list of restrictions that characterize the "margins." Is this list too broad, too narrow, or realistic? Have you seen or experienced some of these restrictions taking place yet? How?

Part I

Reasons for the Return

Chapter 1

The Collapse of Christendom

The church was scarcely freed from the oppression of its persecutors when it had to encounter a trial more terrible perhaps than that of hostility: the embarrassing and onerous protection of the State. – J. R. Palanque[2]

The song is ended but the melody lingers on. – Irving Berlin

Understanding Christendom
The First Three Centuries

The New Testament ends with the mysterious, intriguing, and often baffling book of the Revelation of Jesus Christ to the apostle John. It was written toward the end of the first century at a time when the church was growing numerically, expanding geographically, and beginning to experience systematic persecution across the Roman Empire. These early Christians needed a word of encouragement. They needed a word of affirmation that God is sovereign, that he will finally and completely judge Satan and his dominion of evil, and that he will reward those clothed in the righteousness of Christ with a resurrected life in the new heaven and new earth. However they may have understood the chronology and mechanics of the book's prophecies, they could look forward in faith and hope to their own, and creation's, final redemption. In the midst of daily life, trials, tribulations, and persecutions, they could

---

2   J. R. Palanque, *The Church in the Christian Roman Empire* (1949), 69, quoted in F. F. Bruce, *The Spreading Flame* (Grand Rapids: Wm. B. Eerdmans Publishing Company, 1958), 301.

persevere in their Lord's promise that he is *coming quickly* to judge all (Rev. 22:7, 20).

For the next two and a half centuries, Christianity continued to grow and expand geographically, yet not without struggle and pain. First, Christianity spread throughout the known world. Most Western Christians know about its spread into Asia Minor, Greece, Italy, on to Spain, Gaul, up the Rhine Valley, and eventually into Britain. In this case, as it was in the book of Acts, Christianity's spread through Europe followed the established contours of the Roman Empire.

What is often overlooked, or unknown, by Western Christians is the spread and influence of Christianity in North Africa, and to lands north and east of Palestine. Tradition tells of some of the apostles traveling and evangelizing in Ethiopia, Scythia, in the region of the Caucasus, and even into India. Whether or not these reports are true, they are not necessary to prove Christian communities existed outside the Roman Empire. Christian communities grew in Edessa, Armenia, Mesopotamia, and all the way to Persia. Before the end of the third century, Christianity had even penetrated Arabia and probably had arrived in India.[3]

Second, within the church the content of the gospel was often intensely debated. We read about the earliest debate, which took place at the Jerusalem Council, in Acts 15. As the gospel continued to spread, as churches were planted, and as the apostles' letters were read, taught, and preached, inevitable

---

3   Kenneth Scott Latourette, *A History of the Expansion of Christianity, Vol. 1: The First Five Centuries* (New York: Harper & Brothers Publishers), 91-107 passim. Significantly and encouragingly, Latourette, 116, notes that "The chief agents in the expansion of Christianity appear not to have been those who made it a profession or a major part of their occupation, but men and women who earned their livelihood in some purely secular manner and spoke of their faith to those whom they met in this natural fashion." Martin Marty, *The Christian World: A global history* (New York: The Modern Library, 2007), 74, notes that by the end of the second century "... most [Christian] growth was in Asia Minor and Syria. Europe, which many Western Christians later came to think of as the center of the global Christian community, developed late."

differences of interpretation and application arose. What did it mean and how was it possible that Jesus was truly God and truly man? What were the implications of this for his nature, his relationship with the Father, and for the salvation of humankind? What was the nature of the Holy Spirit and his relationship to the Father and the Son? The reality of transformed lives and the growing recognition of the New Testament canon demanded answers to these kinds of questions.

Answers were not automatic, rapidly formulated, or unanimously accepted. Some ill-conceived answers were that Jesus was not truly flesh but only appeared to be so, or was part of a hierarchy of spiritual beings, or was a special man who was adopted by the Father as Son, or was a special man upon whom descended the Spirit of the Christ. Others claimed that God simply revealed himself at different times as Father, Son, and Holy Spirit, or the Father himself suffered on the cross. Eventually, after the church wrestled with the whole counsel of Scripture, produced a vast body of theological writings, and engaged in important conciliar debates, the Holy Spirit led the church in understanding what we now refer to as orthodox Christianity. These doctrines were then explained and described over the next few centuries in statements accepted by the majority of the church.

Finally, outside the church, periods of persecution existed throughout the empire which served to solidify the commitment of believers and enhance their witness to nonbelievers, including the ruling powers. The earliest believers were no strangers to persecution. The New Testament tells of dispersion and persecution, and much of what the writers address is life in the midst of persecution. The Roman Empire and its rulers objected to the "illicit cult" of Christianity. They realized followers of this cult would not acknowledge Caesar as Lord and were obviously atheists, since they worshipped no visible god.

Furthermore, Christians were accused of practicing cannibalism and even ceremonial incest. Therefore persecution, which varied in both intensity and frequency, periodically increased. Sometimes it was official and widespread while other times it was spontaneous and localized, but it was always irrespective of age, sex, or even position in society.[4]

Christians did not, however, shrink from persecution. Many were martyred for their faith. Others were imprisoned, dispossessed, ostracized, and ridiculed. Still, they held to their faith, sharing and preaching it such that their numbers continued to increase. Persecution did not slow the movement of God, but rather, purified, compelled, and strengthened those who were part of it. Some took up the pen as apologists or defenders of the faith, answering false charges of immorality and explaining true biblical Christianity. More often Christians practiced what they preached and thus became a significant example to others. As instructed by Scripture, they cared for widows and orphans, even while ridiculed by pagans. They excelled in charity, took care of the sick, and treated slaves as equal brothers in Christ.[5]

By the end of the first three centuries of her life, the church had shown in the midst of the worst kinds of tribulations that she was not only capable of survival, but also of victory. This victory, however, was won with spiritual weapons alone. Christians knew there was no need to resort to violence or political machinations because behind the emperors and their persecutions stood Satan himself throwing all his might at the church in order to defeat the gospel.[6] They proved that persecution could not defeat the church nor stymie the gospel. To the contrary, it was in the midst of persecution and living at the margins of society where the content of the gospel was

---

4   Bruce, 161-87 passim.
5   Ibid., 190-91.
6   Ibid., 289.

first tested, commitment to Christ strengthened, and a witness for the gospel proved greater than its challengers. Could the same kind of spiritual victory be possible, however, when the church moved from the margins of society to the center of power and influence?

Constantine

The pagan emperor Constantine consolidated his power in the Roman Empire, in AD 312, at the Battle of the Milvian Bridge. He claimed, however, that victory was granted to him by the direct intervention of the Christians' God. Prior to the battle, he had seen a vision of the cross in the sky and was commanded to mark his soldiers' shields with the monogram of Christ, the Greek *chi* and *rho*. This marked the beginning of his supposed conversion to Christianity and subsequent patronage of the faith.[7]

Feeling indebted to the God of Christianity, acknowledging the growing number of Christians, and needing to politically unify the empire, in AD 313, Constantine declared Christianity the favored religion. Although there were continued periods of favor and disfavor for both pagans and Christians, the situation was never the same. Eventually Christianity was declared the official religion of the empire, and Christendom was established.

Christianity being officially favored was beneficial in many ways. The church appropriated pagan holidays and injected them with new meaning. Clergy were exempted from having to make contributions to the state, church buildings were built

---

7   Ibid., 294. Bruce notes that this "none too happy precedent" of "claiming the sanction of Christianity for warfare," was something that seemed "strangely inconsonant" with Christ. Moreover, there is disagreement among historians as to the sincerity of Constantine's conversion. Bruce, 298, says there "is no reason to doubt the genuineness of Constantine's acceptance of Christianity, in spite of his barbaric outbursts which deface the record of his reign from time to time." To the contrary, Robert A. Baker, *A Summary of Christian History* (Nashville: Broadman Press, 1959), 23, states that it "is hardly conceivable that Constantine really became a Christian," and that "Constantine's adoption of Christianity was more of a political than a religious decision." He wanted to unify the empire by making Christianity the "cement of the empire."

or enlarged, wills could be made out to the church, bishops could handle and decide civil lawsuits, and the copying of the Scriptures was encouraged.[8] In general, the culture was slowly but surely being transformed into a "Christian culture" to such a degree that "Christianity became identified with Greco-Roman civilization."[9]

On the surface, it appeared the kingdom of God had come on earth, displacing the kingdom of men. The problem, however, was that along with favor rained on the church by the Emperor came corruption of the gospel and the church. For one, it meant a considerable number of Christianized pagans entered the church. Through political pressure, family influence, or simply because it had become fashionable, many pagans were baptized and joined the church while keeping their pagan beliefs and practices. Furthermore, the Emperor was allowed to have (or simply took) a part in the internal affairs of the church, including doctrinal decisions, although he was an amateur theologian and rarely understood what he was dealing with. This interference "effectively mortgaged the future of Christian liberty."[10]

The consequence of such a marriage of church and state was that all born into the empire were considered Christians. Inevitably, "Christianity would quickly accommodate the political and cultural impulses of the world,"[11] muddying the message of salvation, seducing the church into practices of power and coercion, and effectively killing the Great Commission missionary mandate.

Growth and Collapse

Christendom was, therefore, in its more formal definition,

8   Latourette, 172-75; Bruce, 295-300.

9   Latourette, 172.

10   Bruce, 295-96. Marty, 42, notes that Constantine was well aware that to "control the empire he had to dominate the church."

11   Michel Pocock, Gailyn van Rheenen, and Douglas McConnell, *The Changing Face of World Missions* (Grand Rapids: Baker Academic, 2005), 165.

the "alignment of Christianity with the state." There existed a symbiotic relationship between the two: the church relied on political power to maintain doctrinal purity, combat those seen as heretical, and enforce sanctions on the "Christian" population. Simply put, obey the church or else. The state, in turn, relied on the church to give "divine" legitimacy and credence to those in power and to the decisions they made.[12] In this context of official Christendom, the faith was often identified with territory. To be a citizen of the realm was to share the faith of the realm while to be outside of the realm was to be either a heretic or a pagan, and, to embrace a different faith within the realm was to be a dissenter, which could be quite dangerous.[13]

This was the status quo for centuries. Certainly, times of tension and disagreement existed between church and state, between popes and kings. Dissenters and dissenting groups survived, but these were usually held in check without much disturbance to the culture. In the end, the marriage between church and state might at times have been an uncomfortable and forced one, but an effective marriage it was.

The Reformation challenged and changed the nature of that marriage, laying the groundwork for its eventual collapse, yet maintaining the marriage. The relationship between church and state may not have been as rigid as it was in Roman Catholic states (and remained for many centuries), but Protestant nations still had state churches with a faith that identified the realm and the culture. However, a reformation movement which questioned established authority and restored the concept of individual salvation apart from membership in an established church encouraged greater individualism and the further questioning of authority.

---

12   Ibid., 165.
13   Timothy C. Tennent, *Invitation to World Missions: A Trinitarian Missiology for the Twenty-First Century* (Grand Rapids: Kregel, 2010), 19. Latourette, 172, notes that the "vast majority of the population of the Empire called themselves Christian."

Consequently, the subsequent period of the Enlightenment highlighted human individuality and liberty, the authority of human reason, and the innate goodness and inevitable progress of humans while rejecting superstitions of the past and the authority of sacred texts and institutions. Severe rifts between science and religion, and philosophy and religion occurred. The inevitable trickle down from academia to art, culture, politics, economics, daily life, and even into the church spelled the eventual doom of Christendom.

As modernity (life defined and fueled by Enlightenment ideals) took hold in the Western world, Christianity was deemed increasingly unreasonable and inconsequential. The Bible was seen as a superstitious ancient text, the church as irrelevant, and Christianity as merely the potential source for ethical behavior. Science, technology, and either empiricism or rationalism, depending on one's philosophical bent, became the ultimate sources of authority.

When these idols of modernity failed to deliver the desired ultimate answers, the inevitable result was postmodernism. Whereas modernity believed in and sought absolute truth through human efforts, postmodernism rejects the notion of absolute truth. Relativism and pluralism reign. Experience and context are ultimate authorities. Christianity is, therefore, just one option among a plethora of spiritualities. Modernity is definitely not dead (witness the rise of the new atheism which is driven by faith in scientific certainty), but it is fighting for its life.

Christendom, therefore, has collapsed, even in traditional Roman Catholic countries. Church buildings in Western Europe are seen as relics and museums of the past. Church attendance has declined to single digit percentages. The church "has been culturally marginalized," and the "old Christendom model has been displaced."[14] The Queen of England still may be

---

14   Pocock, et al, 168.

officially the Defender of the Faith, but no one takes that title seriously anymore. The Pope is still revered globally, but millions worldwide are leaving the Roman Catholic Church, and it is not too flippant to say that his pronouncements are generally viewed as suggestions. Christendom, as a formal church-state relationship, and as the determiner and identifier of Western culture, is dead. It is just that the body has not been buried; or, as the Irving Berlin song says, "The song is ended but the melody lingers on."

Reflections, Lessons, and Consequences

Christendom began to collapse centuries ago. Its influence is still felt and will be for some time. How should we reflect, positively and negatively, on the influence of Christendom and its subsequent collapse?[15]

As already noted, the primary characteristic of Christendom was the symbiotic relationship of church and state, and the close identification of Western culture, good and bad, with Christianity. On the positive side, this provided a foundation for common societal mores. Although these may not have been universally agreed upon or practiced, and some mores may not have been biblically solid, they were generally understood as the acceptable status quo. From these sprang the values that informed common morality, patriotism, politics, education, and the arts. If there happened to be dissent, the church and the state were united as they dealt with those responsible. Consequently, certain worldview, philosophical, and political assumptions could be made which facilitated the founding of schools and universities, hospitals, and other benevolent ministries.

---

15   Please note, however, that I am talking about Christendom and not biblical Christianity or the church when understood as the Body of Christ. I am also definitely not condemning the whole of Western Culture, for there is much to be proud of and thankful for. The concern should be the confusion of biblical Christianity with the culture, whether good or bad aspects, and the melding of state and church power for mutual protection.

Likewise, a monolithic culture allowed for unity in fighting the pagans or even engaging in war with another Christendom nation. After all, the king was the true defender of the faith, he was the monarch according to divine decree and ecclesial affirmation; the people were Christians; and God was definitely on "our" side.

All this religious and political hegemony may have made it easier for the royals, the aristocratic nobility, and the church hierarchy, but it came at a great price.

First, Christendom could only be held together by power. The church and state could only maintain their mutually profitable relationship through power, coercion, and violence. Dissenters had to be silenced, heretics disposed of, rebels stopped, and pagans forcefully converted or killed. Unity of church and state made this a political necessity and a mutually beneficial priority. Such an arrangement, however, led to (and always does) corruption, oppression, and violence at and from the centers of power.

Second, because Europe was "Christian," the general disposition was that the Great Commission had been fulfilled. What about the pagans outside of the realm? Either they were to be defended against (such as Islam) or forcefully converted (the New World). Thus, prior to the beginning of the Modern Missionary Movement at the end of the eighteenth century, the missionary impetus for fulfilling the Great Commission was almost non-existent, with only sporadic exceptions.[16]

Third, such corruption and abuse of power meant that the gospel of Jesus Christ and the prevailing culture had become so syncretized as to be unrecognizable. The Bible, which was in the hands of a few, and the name of our Lord, were used to justify

---

16   Wilbert R. Shenk, "The Culture of Modernity as a Missionary Challenge," *Church between Gospel & Culture*, eds. George R. Hunsberger and Craig Van Gelder, (Grand Rapids: Wm. B. Eerdmans, 1996), 71, notes that the "church of Christendom was a church without a mission." Missions were, he says, "unthinkable" in that context.

any and every political agenda. At the center of Christendom power, Jesus was not the Lamb of God or the Suffering Servant. He was, rather, the Conquering King, and that for the status quo.

Today, we both live in the shadow of Christendom, and are trying to understand how to live missionally in the aftermath of its collapse. Some key aspects of our struggle include:

1. The church has moved from the center to the margins. This is already a fact in Western Europe and Canada, and is more and more so in the United States. Increasing secularism, with its accompanying relativism and pluralism, continues to push the supposed irrelevant church to the side. The church no longer is a major or important partner in power nor does it even have that much cultural influence. The specifics of this will be examined in the next chapter.[17]

2. Paradoxically, however, the non-Western world still sees the West, and America in particular, as a Christian culture and all Westerners as Christians. Christendom's identification of the gospel with Western culture and ways has backfired. Our syncretism confuses non-Westerners, and all arguments made by those who insist that Western countries, or the United States in particular, are Christian nations only worsen the situation. The Muslim in Yemen, for example, looks at our entertainment industry and wonders how "Christians" can behave that way. Missionaries tell of cab drivers playing Michael Jackson music, proudly telling how they, too, listen to "Christian" music. I have a friend, a converted believer from Islam, who once asked me how it was possible that certain things could be believed and

---

17   Pocock et al, 168, note that this "marginalization of Christianity is not surprising to those who understand that the authentic way of Christ, even during Christendom, has always existed on the periphery of popular culture."

practiced – even "allowed" – in America, a Christian nation. I had to explain to him that we are *not* really a Christian nation and that we value freedom even when it contradicts Christian values. It becomes an enormous challenge for missionaries to disentangle culture from the gospel in order to gain a hearing.

3. The good news is that the death of Christendom means the rise of biblical evangelism and missions. Missiologist Timothy Tennent argues that "[one of] the great ironies of history is that only with the death of Christendom can there be a proper birth of evangelism. Christendom has always been effective in producing great numbers of nominal Christians, but it is hopeless when it comes to biblical evangelism."[18] Christendom meant a state church and a Christian culture, so all born into the realm were Christians. Evangelism was passive, and there was no need to defend the faith either within Christendom or to non-Christian worldviews.[19] As pagan lands were later conquered, forced conversion made nominal Christians out of millions of conquered peoples. The collapse of Christendom means that biblical evangelism and discipleship will become, once more, distinguishing marks of the evangelical church.

4. The collapse of Christendom does not mean, however, that Christianity has collapsed! To the contrary, as Christendom unraveled, especially during the twentieth century, the church's center of gravity shifted south. The majority of Christians today are in Africa, Latin

---

18   Timothy C. Tennent, *Theology in the Context of World Christianity* (Grand Rapids: Zondervan, 2007), 181.

19   Tennent, *Invitation to World Missions*, 20.

America, and Asia.[20] The future of Christianity is truly global, just as it was always intended to be.

But, what does Christendom have to do with the United States? We have never had an official state church, so how did its reality shape us and how does its collapse affect us? The American experiment was unique politically and religiously. To that we now turn.

Questions for Reflection and Discussion

1. What are some non-biblical views of Christ you have encountered? How did you respond to them?

2. What are some well-known New Testament passages that address the reality of persecution in the lives of believers?

3. What is your first impression of Constantine's decision to make Christianity the favored religion of the empire? In what ways was this a good decision? In what ways was it a mistake?

4. In what ways is Christendom reflective of biblical Christianity? In what ways is it contrary to biblical Christianity?

5. What evidences do you see of "Christendom" in Western society? In American life?

6. How has the collapse of Christendom been a good thing? How has it been a bad thing?

---

20 Justo L. González, *A History of Christian Thought, Vol. III: From the Protestant Reformation to the Twentieth Century* (Nashville: Abingdon Press, 1975), 430. Phillip Jenkins, *The Next Christendom: The Coming of Global Christianity* (Oxford: Oxford University Press, 2002), notes that this "southern Christianity" will be "far more conservative in terms of both beliefs and moral teaching" and will "retain a very strong supernatural orientation."

Chapter 2

The Fading of
American Civil Religion

The Bible Belt is collapsing. The world of nominal, cultural Christianity that took the American dream and added Jesus to it in order to say, "You can have everything you've ever wanted and heaven too" is soon to be gone. Good riddance. – Russell Moore[21]

In God We Trust – Motto of the United States (as of 1956)

Christendom and the American Experiment
Early Protestantism

Christendom first came to the shores of America with Spanish explorers to what are now Florida and the American Southwest. More influential in American history, British colonists brought Christendom with a Church of England flavor. By the time of the American Revolution, however, European Christendom would be challenged but not thoroughly rejected.

In the beginning, those who came to the colonies were fleeing the oppression, rigidity, and corruption of the established church in England. The story of these Pilgrims, Puritans, and Dissenters is engrained in our national consciousness. We celebrate how they came to American shores seeking religious

---

21   Russell D. Moore, "A Prophetic Minority: Kingdom, Culture, and Mission in a New Era." Inaugural Address as President of The Ethics & Religious Liberty Commission of the Southern Baptist Convention, September 10, 2013. *http://www.russellmoore. com/2013/09/19/a-prophetic-minority-kingdom-culture-and-mission-in-a-new-era/?utm_ source=rss&utm_medium=rss&utm_campaign=a-prophetic-minority-kingdom-culture- and-mission-in-a-new-era&utm_source=feedblitz&utm_medium=FeedBlitzRss&utm_ campaign=mooretothepoint* (accessed 30 September 2013).

freedom, usually conceiving of themselves as God's chosen people, and determined to establish true Christian communities. The reality is a bit more complicated. They did come to escape persecution in England, but were often guilty of the same as some "still hoped to achieve their own variation of the *Corpus Christianum* in America." They did see themselves to some degree as God's people, chosen to replace a corrupt Europe and establish a Christian community, but not all could agree on what that meant. Thomas Hooker founded Connecticut to allow for more tolerance than he found in Massachusetts Bay. Roger Williams founded Rhode Island because he wanted the "civil realm separated from the ecclesiastical." In the end, however, it was clear that American Protestantism would not be comfortable with the church-state coziness of Christendom.[22]

This sense of covenant among America's early Protestants helped shape the United States with mixed results. On the one hand, the sense of mission and destiny for God's chosen people, as historian Martin Marty points out, "led to moral productivity."[23] Human rights, the worth of the individual, and freedom of conscience were grounded in the biblical worldview of these early Protestants. On the other hand, that sense of manifest destiny also led to genocide, slavery, and too often, the imposition of our will on other nations. In these cases, the biblical worldview was twisted to support pragmatic and material gain.

Two extremes should be avoided in evaluating our Puritan background. On the one hand, some pin all our national identity on these early Pilgrims. They argue that the essence or core of American identity is the Christianity of these early

---

22   Glen A. Moots, "The Protestant Roots of American Civil Religion," *Humanitas* Vol. XXIII, Nos. 1 and 2, 2020, 97.
23   Martin E. Marty, "Series Preface," in *Modern American Protestantism and Its World*, Vol. 3, "Civil Religion, Church and State," ed. Martin E. Marty (Munich: K.G. Saur, 1992), x.

settlers, period. When taken too far, America is seen as Israel's replacement in God's plan for history or identified as the perfect expression of biblical Christianity.[24] On the other hand, some secularists ignore or minimize the influence of early Protestantism on the shaping of America. They refer only to the "gospel of commerce"[25] prevalent in the middle colonies and to the Enlightenment values of the Founding Fathers. The reality is that America is the result of the three-fold convergence of a Judeo-Christian worldview (which included religious freedom), the pursuit of financial freedom and material wealth, and modern philosophies growing out of the Enlightenment.

Enlightenment Philosophies

Without a doubt, America's Founding Fathers were a religious bunch. Some were committed Christians, holding to a high view of the Bible and to orthodox doctrines. These could even be described by the more modern term *evangelical*. Many of them, however, were religious and Christian only in the broadest ethical sense, not doctrinally orthodox at all. They were products not only of the nominal Christianity of Christendom, but also of the empiricism of the Enlightenment.

Grounded in the philosophies of Thomas Hobbes and John Locke, empiricists argued that knowledge comes from

---

24   The furthest extreme is seen in the statements of those like Josiah Strong, who circa 1885 wrote that the Anglo-Saxon race, as embodied in America, was destined to colonize the world. The Anglo-Saxon, he said, "excels all others in pushing his way into new countries," and that God is preparing the Anglo-Saxon for the *"final competition of races,"* for we are destined to have "Anglo-Saxonized mankind." Josiah Strong, "America the Embodiment of Christian Anglo-Saxon Civilization," *Church and State in American History: The Burden of Religious Pluralism,* 2d edition, eds. John F. Wilson and Donald L. Drakeman (Boston: Beacon Press, 1987), 137. It is this ethnocentric theology that laid the groundwork for organizations like the Ku Klux Klan. Stephen M. Stookey, "In God We Trust?: Evangelical Historiography and the Quest for a Christian America," *Southwestern Journal of Theology* Spring 1999, Vol. 41, Number 2, 53-54, points out that looking at Puritan America as "normative for the American experience" is to ignore that the Anglican Church "enjoyed preferred status as the established church" from "Maryland south to Georgia," and that the Puritans found themselves confronted by "an ever-increasing unregenerate population."
25   Moots, 99.

experience, either internal or external. When it came to religion, a knowledge grounded in experience would lead to a Christianity restored to "its original reasonable simplicity," for it would get rid of "futile speculations of all sorts of theological scholasticism." That is, getting rid of a history of speculative theological baggage would lead to the most "reasonable form of religion." The result was Deism, or Christianity reduced to its most basic and reasonable elements – doctrines that "could be supported by the proper use of reason."[26] Many of the Founding Fathers, therefore, were not orthodox Christians but Deists who denied revealed Scriptural truths, who denied the Trinity, and who accepted Jesus as not much more than the model man who lived as the best example of the Christian ethic.

Furthermore, the general population was not much better off. As often happens, the intellectual skepticism of the academic world and the elite trickled down to the pulpit and into the pew with unfortunate results. Many colonists, like people of any day, were more concerned and consumed by the demands of daily life and the desire to better themselves financially. By the time of the Revolutionary War, the colonies were at "the beginning of a rapid religious decline" with less "than 10 percent of the population" professing to be Christians.[27] This is amazing because it was not long after the First Great Awakening.

The result was the intersection – the marriage, it could be said – of our Puritan heritage and Enlightenment Deism. This union was not "as strange as it may seem to be," for both shared the assumptions of natural religion and could unite for common political ends. The English Puritans were quite comfortable with "a distinction between the realm of nature and the realm of grace." In nature, God had his "great kingdom, the world." In grace, he had his "special or peculiar kingdom." In nature,

---

26   González, *A History of Christian Thought,* Vol. III, 334-36.
27   Baker, 306.

God rules by "the light of nature and to an outward good and end," while in grace he "rules the Christian by his special revelation in Christ to an inward spiritual end."[28]

Consequently, the public religion of America's Founding Fathers was a natural religion grounded in Enlightenment principles, yet informed by biblical themes and thus ideal for the nature and mission of the new country.[29] Men like Benjamin Franklin, Thomas Jefferson, and even Thomas Paine could exist comfortably in this religious sphere because their God was nature's God. He was known through reason far better than through revelation; he was reasonable, benevolent, and not too demanding, and the man Jesus showed us how to live a good moral life. To the contrary, "spiritual religion" was private and "experienced" and was, in the case of some of the founders, true biblical Christianity.[30] For these, the Bible was God's revelation, Jesus was God incarnate, and humans needed to be redeemed from their sins.

The Founding of a "Christian" Nation

In light of this, was the United States of America founded as or founded to be a Christian nation? The debate over the answer to that question is endless. At one end of the spectrum are those who see every mention of God and every quote of Scripture by the Founding Fathers as evidence of their commitment to biblical Christianity. At the other end are those who focus solely on the Enlightenment worldview of the founders and will admit

28   Winthrop S. Hudson, *Religion in America*, third ed. (New York: Scribner's Sons, 1981), 93.

29   Hudson, 112, notes that there were two versions of the mission of America: One, in which America was to be a "light to the nations," which often meant that we were to be the philosophical and political emancipators of mankind. Two, and closely related, America was to be the "liberator of the oppressed." Unfortunately, too often through our history the mission of emancipator or liberator was carried out from the perspective of a superior "master" or "tutor," often imposed on other nations. We still struggle with this role. How often do we publicly debate whether or not we should be the "world's policeman"?

30   Ibid., 114.

only to a vague cultural religiosity in a few of these men. The truth is somewhere in the middle.

Due to a Christendom environment, a general religious worldview, the prevalence of natural religion, and the acceptance of the Bible by all founders as a beneficial guide for a moral and ethical life, whatever quotes and biblical references by our founders must be seen in their full context. They do not, in and of themselves, express a belief in orthodox Christianity. For example, Thomas Jefferson did say, "I am a real Christian, that is to say, a disciple of the doctrines of Jesus." When read in context, however, and when placed in the context of Jefferson's other writings, it is obvious that he rejected the deity of Jesus Christ and was referring to Jesus' ethical and moral teachings alone.[31] Again, some of the Founding Fathers were biblical Christians, but many were religious men who appealed to a deistic God and quoted Scripture for moralistic reasons and when it served their political purposes, just as they also appealed to John Locke and other philosophers for support when necessary.

To deny, however, that Christianity or even religion in general had a significant place in the founding of America is also to deny history. It was a religious environment, a Christendom environment, and a culture grounded in a Christian ethic. Contrary to what many secularists claim, the founders did not want to exclude religion from the public square. In this respect, Jefferson is once again taken out of context by secularists. His famous statement about a "wall of separation" between church and state was *not* an argument against religion or against religion's presence or influence in government and public life. It was rather an assurance to Danbury Baptists that the government would not encroach on their and others' religious liberty.

---

31   Stephen M. Stookey, "In God We Trust?: Evangelical Historiography and the Quest for a Christian America," *Southwestern Journal of Theology*, Spring 1999, Vol. 41, Number 2, 65.

Furthermore, contrary to popular assumptions, this statement is found nowhere in the Constitution![32]

Secular philosophy played a role, but not the only role in the founding of our nation. As historian Stephen Stookey points out, to "single out one philosophical concept or religious orienta-tion as the sole foundation for America's constitutional origins is a grave mistake."[33] The situation surrounding the writing of the Constitution (which is the context of Stookey's statement) and the founding of America was far more complex than either extreme seems willing or able to acknowledge.[34] In the final analysis, America *was* founded as a religious nation within a broad Judeo-Christian ethic; however, among too many of the founders themselves there is little mention of Jesus Christ, particularly as the incarnate Son of God, Lord and Savior of the world. America was founded, therefore, as a religious nation, but not essentially as a Christian nation.

The Development of Civil Religion
Definitions and Disagreements

What we do have in America and what so many Americans pine for, is a return to a civil religion. The term "civil religion" became part of academic historical and sociological discussion in 1967 after the historian Robert Bellah presented an essay entitled "Civil Religion in America." For Bellah, American civil religion has its foundations in Christianity, but is also composed of a public "set of beliefs, symbols, and rituals" that are "neither sectarian nor in any specific sense Christian." The

---

32   Philip S. Gorski, "Civil Religion Today," Guiding Papers Series, *http://www. thearda.com/rrh/papers/guidingpapers/Gorski.pdf* , notes that for "most of the mid-twentieth century, most American historians characterized the Founding Fathers as 'Lockean liberal' . . . . this reading cannot be fully sustained. Even Thomas Jefferson was influenced by classical republicanism – and Christianity," 8 (accessed 09 October 2014).

33   Stookey, 25.

34   For a more comprehensive discussion of the "Christian America" debate see Terry Coy, *Facing the Change* (Mustang, OK: Tate Publishing, 2013), 215-29.

beginning of this civil religion is found in the "words and acts of the founding fathers" (especially the first few presidents) which shaped the religion's concepts, vocabulary, and content. These men often referred to a clearly unitarian God, who was more interested in morality, order, and law than in love and salvation. This God was, however, actively interested in and guiding the formation of the new nation and its mission with parallels often made to Israel, the Exodus, and to the "chosen nation." Freedom of religion, liberty, justice, equality, and the pursuit of happiness are all themes of this religion, which compels us as individuals and as a nation to carry out God's will on earth.[35]

Scholars are by no means in agreement on the concept of civil religion. There is ongoing debate as to its origins, its definition, its essential components, its influence and impact on American culture, and even whether there really was or continues to be such a thing as a civil religion. Historian Barry Hankins offers what is probably an overly simplistic definition, yet one that serves the purpose of this discussion. He says that civil religion is "the mixing of religion and patriotism until it is nearly impossible to tell where one ends and the other begins." He does explain, however, the five themes found in the development of American civil religion:[36]

1. The idea that America is a chosen nation with a "grand historical purpose."

2. The sense that America is "an agent for bringing in the millennial kingdom."

3. A religious consensus that binds people together.

4. A "fusion of biblical values" that includes a deistic God and no mention of Christ.

---

35   Robert Bellah, "Civil Religion in America," *www.robertbellah.com/articles_5.htm* (accessed 18 July, 2013).

36   Barry Hankins, "Civil Religion and America's Inclusive Faith." *Liberty, www.libertymagazine.org/author/barry-hankins*, 2-3 (accessed July 18 2013).

5. A "historical authentication," meaning that our success, particularly in wars, validates the first two themes.

If these themes are accurately stated, then how has civil religion been manifested in America? Consider that traditionally we have prayed before athletic events, offered a generic prayer in the school house, placed both the Christian flag and the American flag at the front of the church sanctuary, pledged "one nation under God," and printed "In God We Trust" on our money. Furthermore, presidents and other elected officials take the oath of office with their hand on the Bible; witnesses in the courtroom swear truthfulness on the Bible; all presidents from both parties have invoked God's blessing on America, speak of America's place in God's plan, and plead for God's protection when we go to war. These themes are most obvious and most fervently expressed during national holidays such as Independence Day, Memorial Day, Labor Day, and Thanksgiving.

Three things to note about these observations: *First,* whether or not these practices are beneficial to the nation is a matter of debate, but they are not necessarily reflective of biblical Christianity and are often more confusing than anything. Placing the American flag in the church may be patriotic, but it does confuse patriotism with Christianity, the earthly kingdom of men with the kingdom of God. Prayer in school or before a football game may be a good thing, but a generic prayer is not inherently Christian. At best these practices may reflect a Judeo-Christian heritage and offer some religious comfort. They are not necessarily or inherently biblical.

There are, however, those who appeal to 2 Chronicles 7:14 as an admonition for the nation to pray. The problem is that this verse is directed to Israel, the chosen people of God, and not to the United States (unless one accepts theme #1 above). The contemporary *application* is to the church, God's people, who are to pray and can certainly do so on behalf of the nation.

Second, these practices and statements are generally accepted and manifested by both Republicans and Democrats, conservatives and liberals. Conservatives focus on America as God's chosen nation and his instrument for spreading freedom and capitalism throughout the world. Liberals focus more on the themes of justice and peace as found in the Old Testament prophets. Their view of America is one of a blessed nation obligated to share her resources with the world.[37] Conservatives and liberals may disagree on the meaning and extent of a particular expression of civil religion, but neither is willing to capitulate completely to secularism – yet. A cursory reading of presidential inauguration speeches demonstrates that every one of them, regardless of party or personal piety, appeals to the common themes of civil religion.

Third, and paradoxically, while our civil religion is fading (see below) and moving from traditional Protestant themes through a vague religiosity into full-fledged secularism, more and more political candidates, and every presidential candidate, have felt compelled to declare themselves Christian of some sort. Prior to Jimmy Carter, this was never much of an issue, although Thomas Jefferson was accused of being an atheist, and Alf Landon's Catholicism doomed his candidacy. For one, American civil religion expected and assumed every president was "Christian." Kennedy's candidacy and subsequent election forced Protestants to expand their civil religion horizons, but he was still a "Christian" who appealed to God in his inaugural address. In fact, Kennedy's address was what motivated Bellah to study civil religion![38] Since Jimmy Carter's declaration of being a born-again Christian *and* his rejection by the religious right,

---

37   Derek H. Davis, "Competing Notions of Law in American Civil Religion," originally published in *Law, Text, Culture* 5, No.1 (2000): 265-90, posted with permission of publisher at *http://academics.umhb.edu/sites/all/files/academics/documents/CRL/competing_ver_of_law_in_cr.pdf* (accessed 18 July 2013).
38   Bellah, 1.

every president, including Democrats Clinton and Obama, have declared themselves Christians. Whether any of them, including Reagan and the two Bushes, were genuine believers is not the point. The point is that they recognized the importance of religiosity – civil religion – to the American people and knew what was politically necessary.

Civil Religion Begins to Fade

American civil religion is a historical and current reality. It is still relevant in any political, cultural, theological, and sociological discussion. It has been fading though, and will continue to do so. The average Christian (who may confuse biblical Christianity and civil religion) knows this and, as evidence of a growing secular society, points to the absence of prayer in public schools, objections and even prohibitions to praying publicly in Jesus' name, and a growing biblical illiteracy in the general culture. Whatever it may be called, that average Christian would say the culture is no longer what it once was.

American civil religion, therefore, is fading in both content and influence. There are two primary reasons for this:

First, our ever-increasing cultural and religious pluralism has diluted the Christian content of and minimized the need for a civil religion. Although I have argued that America was not founded as a Christian nation, it was greatly influenced by a Christendom worldview, some of the Judeo-Christian ethic, and Western Enlightenment values. Although at times oppressive towards minorities, a fairly homogenous religious culture dominated. The influx of European Catholic immigrants during the late nineteenth and early twentieth centuries forced that culture to be more heterogeneous in religion and ethnicity. The new immigration waves after 1965 brought in millions from non-European nations and/or non-Christian backgrounds. Muslims, Hindus, and Buddhists have changed the cultural and religious makeup of America. Our cultural "mosaic" or "stew" is no longer solely from European Christendom. This growing religious and cultural pluralism means that our heritage of a Christianized civil religion has little appeal and little relevance to more and more new Americans.

Second, the ever-increasing secularization of our society is pushing civil religion, and particularly the "Christian" elements of civil religion, to the margins of culture. Sociologist Phillip Gorski analyzed the relationship between religion and politics, and argues for the historical reality that civil religion has been in competition with both "religious nationalism" and "liberal secularism." The former advocates "total fusion" of the religious and political communities while the latter wants to keep them as separate as possible. In many of our current political debates and the culture wars of the last forty years, the prevailing rhetoric is between these two extreme positions. Radical secularists from the Left are hostile to religion in general and Christianity in particular, arguing that all religion should be, at most, private and disconnected from the public sphere. Religious nationalists on the Right take the concept of covenant nation to heart and seek the fulfillment of America as a Christian nation, if not as an outright theocracy. Civil religionists are in the middle, are the great majority, and see these two spheres as "independent but interconnected."[39]

Gorski's conclusion is that civil religion is a positive thing, because it keeps those two positions at their respective extremes. Perhaps so, however, it appears that the liberal secularist wing is gaining in numbers and influence, which is the topic of the next chapter. Therefore, with increasing religious pluralism and growing secularization, American civil religion is fading.

---

39   Gorski, 7. See also Joseph Blankholm, "American civil religion in the age of Obama: An interview with Philip S. Gorski." *http://blogs.ssrc.org/tif/2012/06/28/american-civil-religion-in-the-age-of-obama-an-interview-with-philip-s-gorski/* (accessed 19 July 2013).

It will not completely disappear anytime soon. It will, however, have less and less of a Judeo-Christian content and be more and more reflective of the "spirit of religious tolerance," which will require references, appeals, and acknowledgment of a non-offending, generic "god."[40]

Benefits and Dangers of Civil Religion

Our American civil religion, especially the more Christianized pre-1960s version, is what many Christians yearn for. It provided a comfortable culture, one which was for the most part either culturally "churched" or at least tolerant and respectful of the church. Many people may not have been born-again Christians, so evangelism was still necessary. The country as a whole, however, was fundamentally "Christian." What were some benefits of that civil religion-dominated culture?

1. Civil religion, like Christendom, served as the "glue" that held the dominant culture together. If minority religions, cultures, and peoples were to succeed at the American way of life, they had to assimilate to, accept, or at least understand and work within the dynamics of the civil religion.

2. Civil religion provided some semblance of a common ground for answers to the questions of authority, morals, and ethics. It also provided a common language that united the country and gave cause for cooperation during periods of struggle, often serving as a linguistic litmus test for politicians and national

---

40   David L. Adams, "The Anonymous God: American Civil Religion, the Scandal of Particularity, and First Table of the Torah," *The Anonymous God: The Church Confronts Civil Religion and American Society*, eds. David L. Adams and Ken Schurb (Saint Louis: Concordia Publishing House, 2004), 26. Alvin J. Schmidt, "Polytheism: The New Face of American Civil Religion," Adams and Schurb, 198, 204, notes that American Civil Religion has shifted "from deism to an increasingly polytheistic posture" and is "no longer the belief in a god-in-general but a syncretistic belief in *many gods-in-general.*"

leaders. In other words, their effective use of the language of civil religion determined their acceptance by the American people.

3. That civil religion glue kept the extremes from dominating the culture. Theocrats and religious utopians generally stayed on the fringe or withdrew to create their own societies. Anarchists and radical secularists lived on the other extreme, relegated to the political margins. The greater majority of Americans lived in the compromised tension of religious liberty for all and the practice of personal daily piety, although often disagreeing over the extent of the first and the appropriateness of the second.

Unfortunately, civil religion also has its dangers:

1. An active civil religion can confuse patriotism and Christianity, or worse, nationalism and Christianity. Jesus and the Bible are appropriated for "our side," regardless of the morality of our side. To be a patriotic American was essentially the same as being a Christian. Although there have been times in our history when we did the right thing and it could be supported by biblical principles, we overlook that the British were "Christian" too. Both the Union and the Confederacy were "Christian." Even as evil as Nazi Germany was, many Germans were "Christian," whether erroneously supporting the regime or actively opposing it.

My point is two-fold: One, although patriotism is a desirable thing for all citizens, we must be careful not to identify Christianity or the gospel with our patriotism. We must not confuse the kingdoms of earth with the kingdom of God. Two, we must remember that there are millions of Christian believers all over the world, even in "enemy" nations, who are citizens of the kingdom of God. They, too, may be patriots. They may be politically conservative, liberal, or uninterested. We may find ourselves at odds with their nation, but that does not make them any less of a Christian, any more than a fellow American believer who differs with us politically is any less of Christian.

2. If a civil religion does become too closely identified with the nation – the earthly kingdom – it can lead to corruption and oppression. A nation that sees itself as God's chosen, correctly or incorrectly, carries a tremendous burden. To see the nation as the liberator, protector, and emancipator of mankind, and of nations, could be a noble vision. The reality is that there is an almost unbearable tension between vision and practice. That noble vision can become too entangled with politics, economic benefits, and national interests, so it becomes an excuse for the expulsion or enslavement of peoples, military adventurism, and political paternalism.

Take for example the Monroe Doctrine of 1823, which warned European powers against interfering in the affairs of the nations in the Western Hemisphere. Although at times the Doctrine was invoked during serious political confrontations (e.g. the 1962 Cuban missile crisis), it was often viewed with skepticism by Latin American countries as a way for the United States to keep Europe out of Latin American so we could exploit those nations ourselves.

Be sure that this is *not* a "blame America first" rant. All nations, including Latin American nations, have their own histories of persecution, oppression, twisted civil religions, and of placing political, military, and economic interests ahead of morals and ethics. Many are worse than anything found in American history. I am, however, an American writing to Americans, and my point is that we must not confuse our patriotism and national interests with the gospel of Jesus Christ.

3. One last consequential danger of civil religion is that it weakens the gospel of Jesus Christ and the call to discipleship. A nation which prays generic prayers, appeals to a generic God, states that it trusts in a generic God, and flippantly thanks God for touchdowns and pop culture awards regardless of personal lifestyle may be called a religious nation. Doing these things, it might be argued, are better than not doing them. Still, the gospel is more than these public utterances and rituals. The kingdom of God is not this kingdom. Being a disciple of Christ, including confession, repentance, forgiveness of sin, and being transformed daily into his image, is not this civil religion. Moreover, the more we argue that our civil religion is Christianity, the more we confuse unbelievers, especially non-Christians from the rest of the world. If what we display in our civil religion is passed off as Christianity, then either Jesus is rejected by one person as too American or superficially accepted by another person in order to become more American.

Conclusion

We are a nation with a civil religion that is both Judeo-Christian and Lockean at its core. It was formally verbalized by our

Founding Fathers as they sought to unify the nation for revolution and subsequent independence. It developed as the nation grew westward, compelled by Manifest Destiny and the need to civilize/Christianize Native American tribes. It was tested and refined during the Civil War as both sides appropriated the best and the worst of civil religion for their respective causes. It united the American people both during questionable wars of choice and during wars of necessity to defend against world dictators. It continues to draw the country together during times of crisis, whether a presidential assassination or a terrorist attack, and during national holidays and celebrations. Its content, however, is becoming more pluralist, more "tolerant," and more secular in tone. It may still be a civil religion, but it is less Christianized and more secular.

Questions for Reflection and Discussion

1. What do you think of when you hear the term "Christian America"? Does this term bring comfort or discomfort? How "Christian" do you think American has been, is, or should be?

2. How have you understood the term "civil religion"? How do you feel about things like American flags in churches, prayer at public events, politicians swearing oaths on the Bible, and politicians invoking the name of God? Do these actions reflect biblical Christianity? Should they be encouraged, discouraged, or what?

3. How should a Christian who is also a patriotic American live and express that "dual citizenship"? Should churches participate in patriotic events? Why or why not? What are some possible ways your church can celebrate patriotic days and yet keep from muddling the gospel message?

4. What should Christians in other countries, especially in those with an anti-American bent, feel about their own nations? How should they express their patriotism?

5. What are some positive aspects of civil religion? Negatives?

Chapter 3

The Triumph of Secularization

If I were a dictator, religion and state would be separate. I swear by my religion. I will die for it. But it is my personal affair. The state has nothing to do with it. The state would look after your secular welfare, health, communications, foreign relations, currency and so on, but not your or my religion. That is everybody's personal concern!
– Mahatma Gandhi

I submit to you that the tolerant society is open to and encouraging of all religions . . . if we look back through history to all those great civilizations, those great nations that rose up . . . and then deteriorated, declined, and fell, we find they all had one thing in common. One of the significant forerunners of their fall was their turning away from their God or gods . . . . – Ronald Reagan

There was a built-in, and it could be argued, quite intentional tension in the American experiment from the beginning. The tension was the marriage of biblical Christianity (or portions thereof) and Enlightenment ideals. The outcome of this uneasy marriage has been the constant tug-of-war over the role of religion in public life, of which the average churchgoer may argue religion is losing to secularism. That belief holds a lot of truth, but the tale of how we got to this point is a bit more complicated and controversial than may first appear.

Secularity, Secularism, and Secularization

In the common view of most evangelical church members, anything connected with "secular" must be opposed to religion in general and Christianity in particular. Christopher Kaiser, however, points out that "biblical secularity" is a positive value. God created the world of space and time for the purpose of "divine self-expression and self-revelation to humanity." Therefore, "time, temporal events, and temporal goals" in the Bible are secular – of the world and created by God for both his use and the use of his creatures. In the biblical view these are not devoid of spiritual or theological meaning. To the contrary, all that exists in creation, whether human or of the natural world, is under a "sacred canopy" of meaning.[41]

Secularism, on the other hand, is the aggressive political movement or "philosophical view of public or social life that affirms that the less public religiosity there is, the greater the benefits for society."[42] This is what evangelicals feel and fear the most – the seemingly intentional and pervasive attack on biblical morals, the integrity and exclusivity of the gospel, and the freedom to believe, practice, and witness to the same.

Secularization is the historical process of moving from the biblical worldview, in which all creation is understood as being sustained through the presence and the power of God to the situation where God and religion are marginalized, their roles redefined and relocated. Academicians debate the details of this process, the definition and the extent of secularization, and even whether it is taking place.[43] For example, European and

41   Christopher B. Kaiser, "From Biblical Secularity to Modern Secularism: Historical Aspects and Stages," *Church Between Gospel & Culture: The Emerging Mission in North America,* ed. George R. Hunsberger and Craig Van Gelder (Grand Rapids: Wm. B. Eerdmans, 1996), 79-80.

42   Charles Mathewes and Christopher McKnight Nichols, "Introduction: Prophecies of Godlessness," *Prophecies of Godlessness: Predictions of America's Imminent Secularization from the Puritans to the Present Day,* eds. Mathewes and Nichols (Oxford: Oxford University Press, 2008), 8.

43   "There is no unified theory of secularization, and some of the mechanisms

American sociologists of religion disagree on how to understand secularization and interpret their respective histories.
Because European countries are grounded in a history of state
churches, sociologists there understand secularization as the
"transfer of persons, things, meanings, etc., from ecclesiastical
or religious to civil or lay use, possession, or control." They say
there is a correlation between the process of modernization and
the decline of religion's influence and control.[44]

American sociologists, working in the context of a country
"already born as a modern secular society," view secularization
not as it relates to society, for that process is "taken for granted
as an unremarkable fact." Secularization to them is a decline of
religious beliefs and practices among individuals.[45] The phrase
"already born as a modern secular society" probably catches
some readers by surprise. Wasn't the United States founded as
a religious country steeped in the Judeo-Christian tradition?
Yes, but the uneasy marriage of religion and Enlightenment
was evidence of the historical process of secularization!

History and Process

Acknowledging multiple models and understandings of the
process of secularization, Kaiser suggests a model of five historical stages in the development of modern secularism from the
eleventh through the nineteenth centuries. Briefly, these are:[46]

Eleventh and twelfth centuries: The power struggle between
church and state leads to the development of the "dialectic of

proposed by secularization theorists seem to remain obscure. In addition, it is not
clear why indicators of 'secularization' are high in some modern societies – for
instance, in many Western European societies – but lower in others such as the
United States, or why some countries that are far less developed than the Western
industrial democracies are more irreligious." "Secularization," *The ARDA: Association
of Religion Data Archives, http://wiki.thearda.com/tcm/theories/secularization/*
(accessed 10 October 2013).

44   José Casanova, "Rethinking Secularization: A Global Comparative Perspective,"
The Hedgehog Review (Spring & Summer, 2006, 8.
45   Ibid.
46   Kaiser, 86-87.

natural and supernatural." As some kings tried to establish power bases free from the Pope's control, they developed their own bureaucracies and legal codes. Although these were independent of Rome, they were not strictly secular. The kings still viewed themselves and their power in theological terms.

Fourteenth and fifteenth centuries: Emerging nation-states and market economies lead to the "construction of uniform space and time." This refers to the establishment of socio-political borders (lines on a map and not necessarily natural borders) and to commerce carried out through legal regulations and national alliances, rather than through traditional relationships.

Seventeenth century: Nation-states stabilize in the post-Reformation period with "the rise of the mechanical philosophy" (all things, including living beings, are like machines and can be understood through simple cause and effect and mechanical processes).

Eighteenth century: The rise of commerce and the popularization of mechanical philosophy led to the "construction of the modern self," which is more and more autonomous. The individual is identified less with family, clan, and tribe but more independent and self-determining.

Late eighteenth and nineteenth centuries: The industrial revolution and advances in transportation restructure communities, increase mobility, and lead to the privatization of religion.

Perhaps even more important is Kaiser's understanding of the content of that historical process. He examines six "aspects" where significant changes occurred during that process. These are:[47]

Socio-political: The emergence of the modern nation-state which led to less interest in and reliance on the authority and direction of church leaders in Rome.

Spiritual: Spirits were disengaged from the objective, public

---

47   Ibid., 87-111.

world, and a clear distinction was made between the supernatural (mostly private religion) and the natural world, which
could be studied and explained apart from any reference to
God. God was available as an explanation for the "gaps" in our
reasonable scientific explanations.

Socio-psychological: Individuals were abstracted and distanced
from their social roles. Individualism and self-actualization
became the ultimate human goals.

Cosmological: The cosmos was de-animated, and matter
was commodified. Humans were completely divorced from
the creation, and matter (nature) was to be used and exploited
without any theological concerns.

Phenomenological: This took the human/nature separation
a step further. The rational mind is the *subject,* which "exists
in splendid isolation." All else is the *object,* devoid of all spirit
and "tones of personality."

Cultural: A person's life patterns transcend tradition, community, and place. In this case, the "homogeneity of local communities" was replaced by multiple worldviews and lifestyles
in towns and cities.

The process of secularization, therefore, has been an historical constant affecting every aspect of individual and community life, moving God and supernatural explanations for the
world to the margins of human knowledge and consciousness.
Religion was pushed out of the realm of philosophy and science
and relegated more and more to the purview of personal piety
and morality. Be religious if you want, but keep it personal.

At what was arguably the culmination of that historical process came the birth of the United States. According to Kaiser's
model, that momentous event was in the midst of the popularization of the mechanical philosophy, the split of the object
and subject, the division of the natural and the supernatural,
and the rise of the autonomous self. The founding of America

as a modern "secular" state was something historically unique. That did *not* mean, however, the abandonment or "disappearance" of religion. It did mean, as evidenced in the majority of our founding documents, the "relocation" of religion into the private sphere of life.[48]

Since that time we have battled over how private that relocation or separation should be. In fact, the most well-known phrase in the battle, the famous "wall of separation" between church and state, is misunderstood by both sides. Secularists see the wall as a way to keep religion in its place – private, out of the public square, and marginalized. Religionists see the wall as a way to protect the practice of religion in both its private and public expressions from encroachment by the state. Religionists say the wall is to protect the free exercise of religion and to prevent the establishment of any one religion, not to eliminate or marginalize it. Whatever one's take is on the famous wall, the fact the metaphorical wall exists points to the United States as "the paradigmatic form of a modern secular, differentiated society." That differentiation has been and continues to be rather "diffused" and fuzzy.[49] Thus, the battle continues.

Implications and Applications

In the end, what does secularization mean for the United States and for the evangelicals in particular? Let me offer the following suggestions:

1. The world is essentially religious. A religious United States is often compared to a secular Europe with the assumption that Europe is the norm. To the contrary, the "U.S. is not the exception, Europe is," with Canada

---

48   Martin E. Marty, *The Modern Schism: Three Paths to the Secular* (New York and Evanston: Harper & Row, 1969), 11.

49   Casanova, 12.

"about halfway between" the two. Furthermore, there has been the sociological assumption that modernity causes or brings about secularization. That assumption is being re-thought or altogether dropped as there are countries far less "modern" than the United States and yet more secular. Modernity actually brings about the interaction of cultures, peoples, and religions. Modern mobility and the transitory nature of people lead to religious pluralism.[50]

2. The American situation is just that. We are quite a religious nation, founded upon a modern secular model where the establishment and official recognition of any particular religion was not an option. That was a good thing; however, therein lies the rub! The unintended consequences were twofold: One, we live with a constant tension between state and church, private piety and public religion. We strain to understand the role religion plays in society. Two, the stage was set for religious pluralism, because the free exercise of religion applied to all religions.[51] As would be expected, that growing pluralism only adds to the tension between the religious and the secular, and perhaps paradoxically, the secular is winning. That is, we are not becoming less religious, but the

---

50   Peter Berger, Grace Davie, and Effie Fokas, *Religious America, Secular Europe? A Theme and Variations* (Surrey, England: Ashgate Publishing, 2008), 9-11. The *Association of Religious Data Archives* also notes that "the modernization theory of secularization has been modified." Kaiser, 13, says that the "postulated intrinsic correlation between modernization and secularization is highly problematic."

51   John L. Allen, *The Global War on Christians* (New York: Image, 2013), 252-56, notes that in the United States we like to blame secularism for the decline in religiosity, while in other parts of the world Christians actually want more secularism as a defense for religion! That is, a more secular society brings with it more religious freedom.

"boundaries" are being "relocated, drastically pushing religion into the margins and into the private sphere."[52]

3. As Americans we feel that growing secularization is in large part due to the prevalence of secularism as a movement in academia, mass media, and the entertainment world. In an article for *The American Spectator*, Mark Tooley notes that America "*seems* more secular" because cultural elites are today more secular than they were a hundred years ago. At that time college presidents and faculty, media publishers and editors, and other cultural leaders were either "churchmen" or tolerant toward religion. Today the cultural elite, and particularly those in broadcasting and entertainment, are secular at best and often hostile to religion and especially to evangelical Christianity. Because they control the outlets, their voices and their influence are disproportionate to their actual number.[53]

4. Consequently, the situation is thus:

- We were a nation founded in the midst of Christendom and at the intersection of biblical Christianity and Enlightenment ideals.

- We were both a religious nation and the first modern secular nation. We were secular in the sense that we did not have a state religion and built into our founding documents the "separation of church and state" – however that may be interpreted.

- That stated and expected separation implied and

---

52   Casanova, 11. Casanova, 13, also notes that "modern traits . . . are not developed necessarily in contradistinction to or even at the expense of tradition, but rather through the transformation and the pragmatic adjustment of tradition."

53   Mark Tooley, "A Secularizing America?" *The American Spectator*, http://spectator.org/archives/2012/10/10/a-secularizing-america/print (accessed 10 October 2013).

encouraged the privatization of religion. Public
religion was primarily civil religion, the content
of which was a mild form of Judeo-Christian theology, but which has become both more generic
and pluralistic.

- While we have grown more politically, culturally, and
religiously pluralistic, secularization has increased.
Religion in general and evangelical Christianity in
particular have been pushed further to the margins. Those individuals and churches that hold to
specific evangelical beliefs and practices will find
themselves free to worship as long as it is private.
Having a prophetic voice in public policy and social
issues or engaging in personal evangelism will be
seen as intolerant, hateful, and will probably be
subject to legal penalties in the future.

Although we are a religious world and a religious nation,
secularization is a growing global phenomenon.[54] The evangelical Christian feels the pressure from all sides. On the one
side, religious pluralism is growing. Increasing diversity in
belief and practice demands a voice and a place in an open
and free society. Unfortunately, inevitable religious clashes will
occur. On the other side, secularism rules both academia and
popular culture. The evangelical Christian feels that pointed
hostility daily. What are we to do? There are some lessons to
learn from church history and from global Christianity about
life in the margins. Before those are examined, the evangelical
Christian must understand and confront the issue of knowledge and authority.

---

54   Secularization is certainly not equally in force around the world, but the very
fact that there is a rise in religious fundamentalism, whether Christian, Jewish,
Muslim, Hindu, or Buddhist, demonstrates a strong reaction to real or perceived
secularization. Kaiser, 84, notes that the rise of fundamentalism "can be viewed as
a concomitant of secularization rather than an exception to it."

Questions for Reflection and Discussion

1. How have you understood "secular" and "secularism"? What are some evidences you have seen and "felt" the triumph of secularization?

2. Are there any positives to having a secular society? What are the alternatives?

3. How should a Christian live in an increasingly secular society? How can the church *be* the church in the midst of secularization?

4. How have you seen increasing religious pluralism in America? Is this a good thing or not? How should the church respond?

5. In the midst of growing secularization and religious pluralism, what are some changes in attitude, ministries, or programs your church needs to make? What should your church do to reach this ever growing mission field?

Plan for Action – Part 1

The Church/Religion – Culture/State Relationship

Much of what we have been discussing involves the relationship between culture (which includes the state) and the church (or religion in general). It is probably obvious that there are several understandings of what this relationship should be or could be. It has also been an issue for centuries and continues to be a daily debate in our country. The marginalization of the church is definitely a state/culture—church issue. In some cases the marginalization will be an official or legal action. In other cases, it will simply be the "mood" of the culture, unofficial but no less real. Consider the following diagram as you think about what marginalization of the church may mean for you:

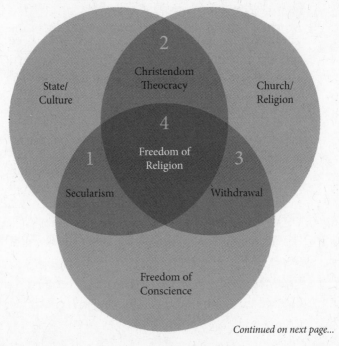

Continued on next page...

1.	3.
• Secularism	• Withdrawal
• Marginalization of Religion/Church	• Fortress/Christian Ghetto mentality
• Potential oppression by State	• Utopian communities
• Limits on freedom of religion	• Rejection of State/ Government as evil
2.	4.
• Christendom	• Freedom of religion
• Civil Religion	• "No establishment" and "free exercise" tension to be maintained
• State Church	
• Religious Nationalism	

1. In which quadrant have we been historically in the United States? What was the intent of the founders?

2. How have we historically drifted into other quadrants? What are some advantages or disadvantages of the other quadrants?

3. Where do we seem to be headed now?

4. How could ministry and mission change if we find ourselves in quadrants 1, 2, or 3?

5. How would your life and your church's ministry change if we were completely in quadrant 1? What can you do to prepare for it?

Part II

Preparing for the Return

Chapter 4

Cling to Authority

The life stance of Humanism – guided by reason . . . we affirm the following: Knowledge of the world is derived by observation, experimentation, and rational analysis . . . . Humanists recognize nature as self-existing . . . Ethical values are derived from human need and interest as tested by experience . . . The responsibility for our lives and the kind of world in which we live is ours and ours alone.
– Humanist Manifesto III[55]

The post-Christian narrative is radically different; it offers spirituality, however defined, without binding authority.
– Al Mohler[56]

The Reality of Authority

All humans are subject to authority. Even the most rebellious, anti-authoritarian individual submits himself to some type of authority. Authority can be defined as that which has power and influence over how a person orders and directs his or her life. It is what a person appeals to, relies on, or defers to when making decisions. Authority may be external or internal, formal or informal, recognized or unconscious, voluntary or coerced, rational or irrational, and certainly natural or supernatural. Although there may be varieties, levels, and different

---

55   *http://americanhumanist.org/Humanism/Humanist_Manifesto_III* (accessed January 3, 2014).
56   Quoted in Jon Meacham, "The End of Christian America," *www.newsweek. com/meacham-end-christian-america-77125*, 4 (accessed January 2, 2014).

sources of authority in a person's life, usually one is ultimate and overriding.

As evangelical Christians, we must answer the question "What authority will we cling to?" What is the authority we will submit to as we are shoved to the margins of society? Should we fall back on pre-modern concepts of authority, hang onto modern tenets of authority, or accept post-modern denial of ultimate authority? During these three eras of Western history, the grounds of authority have shifted numerous times, always with consequences for the Christian understanding of knowing and arriving at truth.

Pre-modern World

Early Christians rebelled against Roman imperial authority by declaring that Jesus and not Caesar was Lord and the teaching of the apostles was authoritative in their lives. They believed this to the point of persecution, and even death. Whatever the prevailing Hellenic philosophies may have been and whatever fierce temporal power Rome possessed, none of it stood up to the ultimate authority of the gospel of Jesus Christ. This meant that truth, meaning, and any explanation of the working of the cosmos, was grounded in religious authority, and specifically the revealed Word of God.

As the canon of Scripture was being recognized by the early church, religious authority began to shift from the oral tradition to the written Gospels and Epistles, but not completely. Along with the written Word, the "apostolic teaching" of those bishops "who served in direct succession" to the apostles was considered as "key to interpretation of the Scriptures." Dependence on the tradition (understood as teaching) of the Roman Catholic Church grew throughout the Middle Ages until it was on a par with the authority of Scripture.[57] Regardless of emperors,

---

57   James Leo Garrett, *Systematic Theology, Vol. 1* (Grand Rapids: Wm. B. Eerdmans, 1990), 170-71.

disagreements between bishops, fights between popes and kings, and competing pagan religions, authority for all of life rested in the revealed will and Word of God in Scripture and through the church.

This does not mean that religious authority was not challenged. Whether it was the cultural impact of the Renaissance, the conciliar movement, or individuals such as Wycliffe, John Hus, Henry VIII, Copernicus, Galileo, and Kepler, the extent and legitimacy of Church authority was often questioned, usually over specific interpretations and often with devastating consequences for the questioner. Generally speaking, however, these were not rejecting the ultimate authority of Scripture or the Lordship of Christ, but differed from ecclesiastical authorities on interpretation and meaning in matters of political governance, science, and the nature of Scripture.

The Reformation changed the understanding of religious authority to a significant degree. Although Protestant leaders understood authority differently, they argued for either the authority of *sola Scriptura* or *suprema Scriptura*. Creeds, confessions, and patristic or medieval writers could inform and assist in scriptural interpretation, but in no way were they authoritative. In every case, the Bible superseded any church tradition or any proclamation from an ecclesial leader. In matters of nature, science, and the workings of the universe, it was still God's creation. Truth was still God's truth and was to be discovered through reading and understanding his written Word.

Modern World

The ongoing process of secularization discussed in the previous chapter meant a shift in authority. Knowing, finding the truth, and the authoritative grounds for declaring what was true moved from what was external to humans (the religious and the revealed) to what was internal and inherent in humans, namely reason and experience.

Reason

As Western civilization moved from the pre-modern to the modern age, there was an "epistemological turn," a philosophical move in how knowledge and truth were apprehended. The "locus of authority" moved from the supernatural – from revelation and religious authority – to "autonomous human reason." Belief in God was still a possibility, but it was to be grounded in rationality rather than in "the necessity of divine revelation." Knowledge, truth, and all of reality were to be discovered and explained by reason and by the scientific method.[58] Furthermore, this rational access to God (or any truth) was universal. Everyone had reason, everyone could use it, and everyone could gain access to the knowledge of God without the need for any particular revelation by God.[59]

Authority, therefore, rested not in revelation or in the supernatural. It was grounded in the rationality of human beings and in our ability to know and prove truth with the kind of certainty and objectivity found in mathematics. Under the authority of reason, anything outside of that certain realm is untrustworthy and to be doubted.[60]

Empiricism

Another way to gain knowledge is on the basis of experience. In this view, humans are born with a mental *tabula rasa* or blank slate. All that is known is based "on experience through the

---

58   Stewart E. Kelly, *Truth Considered & Applied* (Nashville: B & H Academic, 2011), 12-13.
59   Alister McGrath, *A Passion for Truth* (Downers Grove: InterVarsity Press, 1996), 88. For the rationalist "[h]uman nature and rationality [are] independent of its specific historical, social, cultural or chronological location," 165.
60   Lesslie Newbigin, *Truth and Authority in Modernity* (Valley Forge, PA: Trinity Press International, 1996), 7.

traditional five senses." The world can and must be observed neutrally and dispassionately, the data measured and analyzed; then certain, objective knowledge is possible.[61] It is from experience or empirical data that we derive ideas and concepts. These are "dependent on experience," and thus all "knowledge must also be dependent on experience." Ideas, knowledge, and truth, therefore, are not inherent in humans or human nature.[62] Authority rests on human senses and ability to objectively process and interpret the data received.

Modern Authority and the Christian

To rely on reason and experience for knowledge *to some degree* is not a bad thing for the Christian. First, the rational processes of the mind, logical analysis, rational explanations and proof, and the dynamic of doubt and questioning is part of what it means to be human. It is also part of what it means to be a Christian believer. We want our faith to be reasonable and to make sense. We want to be able to explain our faith with coherence and logic. We can and do rely, however, on our God-given reason as a secondary source of authority and not the primary or ultimate source. This is for two reasons: One, because we are fallen human beings and cannot fully trust either our reason or our experience. Two, because there are aspects of our belief that involve mystery and faith, explanations of which come not from our human reason but only from revelation. There are facts, evidences, and knowledge which make sense only to one who is "spiritual," i.e.: regenerated and indwelt by the Spirit of God. On the one hand, we don't want to fall into an anti-intellectual and blind faith only religion. It is not necessary, will not communicate to the world, and is open to unnecessary

---

61   "Empiricism," *The Oxford Companion to Philosophy*, ed. Ted Honderich (Oxford: Oxford University Press, 1995), 226.

62   Norman L. Geisler and Paul D. Feinberg, *Introduction to Philosophy: A Christian Perspective* (Grand Rapids: Baker Books, 1980), 113-14.

criticism. On the other hand, we have to take care not to fall, even as believers, into the trap of excessive rationalism. In this case we may rely too much on our need and ability to rationally understand and explain God's revelation, overlooking the reality of mystery and faith.

Similarly, human experience – what we see, observe, and measure – is also a source of authority for truth *to a certain degree*. This is how we do science. We observe, sense, and measure the world. The data is analyzed and interpreted. We gain further knowledge of reality. Experience cannot be, however, our only nor our primary source for knowledge and our ultimate authority for truth. Empirical observation takes place in a fallen world by fallen human beings. It can inform, adjust, and confirm knowledge and truth, but cannot be our ultimate authority in determining truth.

Post-modern World

As it is with any cultural or social movement, no clear delineation exists between the end of one era and the beginning of another. In the case of the move from modernity to post-modernity, we are talking of overlapping eras. As modernity dies a slow death in the Western world, post-modernity gains in influence (pre-modernity is still the status in parts of the world, and some may go straight to post-modernity due to globalization and a flat world).

The modern experiment grew out of the Enlightenment and advocated that ultimate and objective truth could be found through human reason and experience. The autonomous self was thus elevated to the center of the world and knowledge about the world, which has the potential to be certain, objective, and even absolute. Reason and experience manifested themselves in objective science and technology, which would result in the inevitable progress of the human race. Anything religious, whether personal faith or supposed revelation, was to be tested and confirmed by reason and experience. Thus, revelation, mystery, the miraculous, and a personal God were minimized or outright rejected.

Post-modernity is a reaction to the failure of modernity (some would say it is the extreme and inevitable result of modernity). The certainty of modernity was shattered by two World Wars. Its misplaced faith in science and technology led to the threat of nuclear holocaust, pollution and ecological disaster, and the depersonalization of human beings. This means, says the post-modernist, that objective and absolute truth is a myth and to claim such an absolute truth or metanarrative (big story) is oppressive and an act of violence. History is replete with the violent power of the metanarrative – of those who claimed objective power, knowledge, and authority. Witness the oppression of women, the enslavement of Africans, global colonization, forced conversion to Christianity in the New World, and the regular ethnic cleansing of minority peoples. Truth? Authority for making any claims over life, morals, and ethics? For the post-modernist, such authority is found in two sources, although a post-modernist would not like to use the word "authority," as it implies oppression against the "other."

Culture and Community

This is the move from modern, rational, objective reality to postmodern, relative construction. The postmodern rejects the notion of absolute, objective truth, whether found in reason, experience, or revelation. The post-modern is also not as concerned about the autonomy of the individual. The community – the social group of language, values, and beliefs – is more important.

Therefore, truth, or better said *truths*, are relative and are constructions of culture and community. No objective truth exists out there to be discovered, and then imposed oppressively over all people. Instead, many relative truths are part of and constructed by different communities and cultures, none of which are to be imposed on other communities and cultures. Post-moderns have no problem believing these many truths can exist side by side. Relativism and pluralism reign, for the question is not the correctness or accuracy of these truths, but their viability and pragmatic outcome.[63] These are not, however, grounded in the individual's personal preferences as they were in late modernity, but in the experience and values of the community. Truth is not absolute and discovered by the rational and objective individual, but relative and constructed by the local community.[64]

Personal Experience

This is the move from modern, empirical, objective reality to post-modern, experiential relativism. The Enlightenment empiricist believed certain, objective, and absolute knowledge or truth could be arrived at through observation and experience. Modern man had the potential not only to reason but also to observe correctly and objectively. Grenz characterizes this proud human "as Descartes's autonomous, rational substance encountering Newton's mechanistic world."[65] Knowledge and

---

63   Michael Pocock, "Christ Centered Epistemology: An Alternative to Modern and Postmodern Epistemologies," *The Centrality of Christ in Contemporary Missions*, eds. Mike Barnett & Michael Pocock, Evangelical Missiological Society Series Number 12 (Pasadena, CA: William Carey Library, 2005), 70, notes that "Postmodernism will not accept the superiority or correctness of any religious position beyond its value for the individual."

64   Stanley J. Grenz, *A Primer on Postmodernism* (Grand Rapids: Wm. B. Eerdmans, 1996), 15, says that the "relativistic pluralism of late modernity was highly individualistic; it elevated personal taste and personal choice as the be-all and end-all. Its maxims were 'To each his/her own' and 'Everyone has a right to his/her opinion.' . . . The postmodern consciousness, in contrast, focuses on the group. . . . As a result, postmodern relativistic pluralism seeks to give place to the 'local' nature of truth. Beliefs are held to be true within the context of the communities that espouse them."

65   Ibid., 3.

truth were out there and just waiting to be discovered by us highly capable, rational, and objective individuals.

To the post-modern this is maximum arrogance, an indisputable criticism after the political, economic, ecological, and technological disasters of the twentieth century. As noted, for the postmodern, truth is not absolute, but locally constructed. It is plural and relative. Knowledge and truth are still grounded in experience, but it is not the same experience of the empiricist. The empiricist sought knowledge outside of himself, objective and certain. He discovered it through keen, scientific observation. For the postmodern, experience is subjective and personal yet grounded in community. It is developed or constructed in community through deeply personal experience. Truth is therefore niche truth. Different communities build their own truths and never consider that theirs is above, better, or truer than another. Much less should it ever be imposed on another person or community.[66]

Post-modern Truth and the Christian
The mistake many Christians make is to automatically reject the relativism and pluralism of post-modernity and uncritically hang on to many tenets of modernity. There is much in modernity to hang onto; however, the post-modern is right to criticize the hubris of the modern man. The belief that humans could be objective and grasp, out of their own reason and experience, objective knowledge and truth is not biblical. This confidence was grounded in the belief of the innate goodness and objective abilities of humans, which simply overlooked or

66   A somewhat oversimplified but still true way to express relative truth is stated by Dennis Prager, a practicing Jew, in Aaron Cline Hanbury, "New era in U.S. culture assessed by panel," *www.bpnews.net/printerfriendly.asp?id=41942* (accessed 3 February 2014). He notes that "'We live in the age of feelings'. . . citing abortion rights as the greatest example of individual feelings guiding contemporary morality. The unborn child's worth is 'entirely dictated by the feelings of the mother. It is an unbelievable statement of narcissism, which is what happens when there is no transcendent morality.'"

rejected the biblical doctrine of the fall. Although taking it too far, the post-modern does remind us to be humble and take into account the real influence of culture, experience, and perspective as we seek, verbalize, and pronounce truth.

But post-modern relativism is not the only alternative. There is a truer and safer ground between the Scylla of modernity and the Charybdis of post-modernity.[67]

The Church at an Authority Crossroads
Secularization and the Decline of Religious Authority

The collapse of Christendom, the fading of American civil religion, and the triumph of secularization means the collapse of authority. Al Mohler is correct when he notes that this is a spiritual age, but one "without binding authority." God is not dead; however, we are seeing the "birth of many gods," which reflects post-modern pluralism, the construction of one's own spirituality and spiritual truth, and the emphasis on "tolerance."[68] Sociologist Mark Chaves insists that our understanding of secularization needs to completely change. It is not "the decline of religion, but . . . the declining of religious authority," particularly as it refers to the "declining influence of social structures whose legitimation rests on reference to the supernatural."[69] Simply put, religion is becoming more and more privatized. Religion is being relocated. According to secularization, it no longer belongs in the social or political spheres, but only in the private lives of individuals. Religion is still alive, but there is a definite decline in religious authority.

---

67 That is, between the proverbial rock and a hard place. Scylla and Charybdis were mythical sea monsters (whirlpools in later legend) on opposite sides of the strait of Messina off the coast of Italy. Ships had to sail between them or risk being caught up by one or the other.

68 Quoted in Meacham, p.4.

69 Mark Chaves, "Secularization as Declining Religious Authority," *Social Forces* (March 1994): 72(3):749-774 *www.majorsmatter.net/religion/readings/secularization. pdf* (accessed on December 18, 2013).

We are living in an age that rejects the certainty and absolutism of the rationalist and empiricist. No metanarrative, whether of religion, reason, or science is accepted. Truth is local, which implies that ethics are relative and open to change. Religious revelation and experience are accepted, but they, too, are constructs of personal experience and the community and only semi-authoritative. That is, they are true, but only true for you.

The Choice of the Evangelical Christian

As evangelical Christians face these historical and philosophical realities and their implications for church, ethics, and culture, we return to the question, "What authority will we cling to?"

The Bottom Line

Evangelical Christians agree that the Bible is inspired, authoritative, dependable, and trustworthy, with all that is needed for faith and life. We may define and debate the exact meaning and mode of inspiration, but we agree that God's Word is our final authority for guidance, direction, and decision making in life. We may disagree on our hermeneutical approach, the specific exegesis of a passage, and the application of a particular teaching to our lives, but we agree that the starting point is the written Word of God.

This bottom line should produce both confidence and humility. We are confident that God has not only spoken, but spoken to us, and we can know accurately what the truth is. We are humble because we are aware of textual difficulties, translation differences, diverse hermeneutics, and especially our own sinfulness and limitations. The evangelical Christian, therefore, appeals to the authority of Scripture based on premodern, modern, and post-modern understanding of authority.

With the pre-modern person, we agree that the Bible is the revealed Word of God. That Word was revealed in many ways:

Prophets spoke from God (2 Pet. 1:21); Jesus spoke the words God gave him (John 17:8); Paul wrote letters recognized as Scripture (2 Pet. 3:16); and John experienced a direct vision of the risen Jesus (Rev. 1:1, 12-13). In every case, it is an authoritative word, applicable to the first hearers/readers and applicable to us today. We may struggle with understanding the original meaning and its current application, but we must cling to the Bible as the ultimate authority that judges all other claims to authority.

With the modern person, we agree that reason and experience are real and are to be used as tools. God gave us the ability to think and analyze (Lk. 14:28-32), to design, plan, and build (consider the tabernacle, the temple, Solomon's projects, and the walls of Jerusalem) and to observe and measure the world (1 Kings 4:29-34). Unlike the modern, however, we do not cling to reason and experience as ultimately authoritative. They are to be understood and practiced as from God and within his sovereign rule. They are gifts from him and not inherent in us nor inherently good. With the preacher of Ecclesiastes, we know that all reason and experience is vain and "wearies the body" if not grounded in the fear and obedience of God (Ecc. 12:12-13).

This "moderated" modernity thus rejects the blind authoritarianism of the pre-modern, which was often grounded in the politics and power of church leaders rather than in Scripture. It also rejects the assumption of and the aspiration to be the modern autonomous individual. Faith and the discovery of truth are individual; however, in the Bible the individual is always understood to exist in community, whether family, clan, tribe, nation, or as a member of the Body of Christ. Faith and truth are best discovered and practiced in community.

We also agree with the modern that there is absolute, objective, and certain truth. There is a metanarrative – a story – which encompasses all reality and answers all ultimate questions about life. That is God's story as revealed in his written Word and manifested historically and perfectly in the life of Jesus Christ. This is the authority we cling to.

With the post-modern, however, we agree that we are all, to some degree, constructs of our environment and our community, whether family, race, culture, or nation. Although there is an objective and absolute truth we strive to comprehend and practice, we are not objective. As fallen human beings, we must humbly acknowledge our limitations, our biases, and our perspectives. Therefore:

1. Absolute truth is a reality. It is found in the revelation of our Trinitarian God. He acted in the history of Israel; the incarnation of the Son perfectly revealing the Father, and in the Holy Spirit-inspired writings of the sixty-six books of the canon.

2. Absolute truth is not just information about God. Absolute truth is found in the person and work of Jesus Christ. This means we can hold to the exclusivity of Jesus Christ and argue that his story is *the* story, or metanarrative, that answers all stories.

3. We can know truth sufficiently, correctly, and with certainty. We cannot know truth exhaustively or perfectly, because our sinfulness, our culture, and our experience get in the way. This is not reason for despair, but reason for faith and humility.

4. We cling to the authority of the Bible with confidence. We acknowledge textual, translation, and interpretation difficulties, but we can trust the Bible in our hands.

5. Although we hold to the priesthood of all believers and the freedom for each believer to read and interpret the Scriptures, we believe that the best reading,

interpreting, and application is done in community. We need each other. On the one hand, we must avoid incorrect hyper-individualism. On the other hand, we want to avoid group-think. Trusting and listening to the Holy Spirit, respecting and listening to others, and letting the plain sense of Scripture judge all of our perceptions, perspectives, and interpretations, we move closer to the true understanding and the best application.

Conclusion

As we are moved closer to the margins of society and culture, we will have to make a decision about ultimate authority. Will it be something in humanity, whether reason or experience? Will it be culture itself – the prevailing mood, the preference of the majority, or the path of least resistance? Or, will it be what the marginalized church has always clung to – the living, authoritative, trustworthy Word of God. We must cling to it and its authority, always willing ourselves to be judged, rebuked, and corrected by its teachings. We learn from other sources of authority. We listen and consider the claims of other authorities. But in the end, when push *will* come to shove, we cling to the authority of the Bible, no matter the cost.

Questions for Reflection and Discussion

1. What are some sources of authority people appeal or cling to?

2. What are some benefits of reason? Of empiricism? What are their limits and dangers?

3. What are some contemporary attitudes toward authority? Toward truth? Toward absolutes?

4. Think about your own experience – education, work, culture. What are some sources of authority in these realms? What about your own life and church? Have you ever noticed a discrepancy between what is claimed as authority (the Bible) and what is actually the authority?

5. Discuss the pre-modern, modern, and post-modern views of authority. How do they affect Christians? How should they affect the worldview of Christians?

6. How can today's parents teach their children about the Bible's authority? What are some obstacles, challenges, and objections they may run into?

7. How would you respond to someone who appeals ultimately to what is "reasonable"? To what can be observed?

Chapter 5

Learn from History

On that day a severe persecution broke out against the church in Jerusalem, and all except the apostles were scattered throughout the land of Judea and Samaria.
– Acts 8:1 (HCSB)

Perhaps the most spectacular triumph of Christianity in history is its conquest of the Roman Empire in roughly twenty decades. – Ralph Winter[70]

The Original Marginalized Church

At his ascension, the Lord Jesus commanded his disciples to make disciples of all nations or peoples (Matt. 28:19) which included those in Jerusalem, Judea, Samaria, and to the ends of the earth (Acts 1:8). Before the church could fully implement the Acts 1:8 strategy, a great persecution broke out. This caused the dispersion of the believers, and both voluntary and involuntary sharing took place forming an Acts 8:1 church. The gospel began to spread through the dispersion resulting from persecution.

One of the lead persecutors raging against the followers of Jesus was Saul. This Saul was the worst of sinners (1 Tim. 1:15). He was converted on the road to Damascus and ended up with Barnabas in Antioch teaching large numbers of believers. Irony of ironies (God does have a sense of humor), this church

70   Ralph D. Winter, "The Kingdom Strikes Back: The Ten Epochs of Redemptive History," *Perspectives on the World Christian Movement: A Reader*, eds. Ralph D. Winter and Steven C. Hawthorne (Pasadena: William Carey Library, 1981), 141.

in Antioch was started by some of the very believers who had been scattered as a result of the persecution back in Jerusalem during the murder of Stephen, in which Saul had participated (Acts 11:19). Both Saul (now Paul) and Barnabas were sent out as missionary church planters across the known world by this missionary sending Antioch church.

The result was a world turned upside down by the message of the gospel of Jesus Christ. Whether it was Paul and his team of missionaries, the other disciples, or everyday Christians like Priscilla and Aquila, Lydia, or others, a socially, culturally, and politically marginalized and persecuted minority proclaimed and lived out their faith.

Being a marginalized minority was never easy. The New Testament tells of intermittent persecution of early Christians, instigated first and primarily by Jewish opposition to the claim of Jesus as their Messiah. As mission efforts expanded throughout the Roman Empire, occasional persecution arose from pagans, albeit more often for economic reasons than anything else (Acts 16:16-21; 19:23-27). As the church grew, imperial policies began to change, at first locally, but later, more officially and broadly.

Although Christians were either tolerated or ignored by the Roman authorities for the first three decades after the resurrection of Christ, that began to change in AD 64 when Nero blamed both Jews and Christians for the fire that destroyed much of Rome. The key issue for Rome was a political one. The empire had to be held together at all costs. Regional religions were tolerated as long as they fit into Roman multi-theism or were willing to also acknowledge the supremacy of the emperor. Worship of the emperor and the subsequent declaration that "Caesar is Lord" was the religious glue of the empire. For Christians, this demand was unacceptable. Only Jesus was Lord. The Romans interpreted the Christian refusal to acknowledge the Lordship of Caesar as disloyalty and a threat to the unity of the empire.

For the first three centuries of the Christian era, believers were accused of being secretive (and thus being up to no good), superstitious, and atheistic (for rejecting Rome's gods). Romans thought they were cannibals (their talk of eating the body and drinking the blood) who practiced child sacrifice and all kinds of immorality. Subsequent persecution was not a constant and empire-wide, but it was always serious and life threatening. Whatever the situation at any moment, Christians were always in a precarious and dangerous position. For the leaders of the empire, persecution was "a matter of policy in defense of the integrity of the state."[71]

What can be learned from the original marginalized church? Why did it grow? How did these early Christians survive and even prosper under such uncertain and dangerous circumstances? There are significant and complex political, sociological, cultural, and economic dynamics of the Roman Empire which are integral to any discussion of its fall and subsequent formal acceptance of Christianity. However, focusing on the early Christ followers themselves we find that:

1. They firmly held to the exclusive demands of their message. The early Christians were not willing to suffer and possibly die as martyrs for a philosophy, an ethical system, or an open and inclusive religion. Their founder was not one who could be one among others or incorporated into other belief systems. Jesus Christ was the one and only Lord, the only name under heaven that saves. Their Lord was the only begotten Son of God, who suffered and died for the forgiveness of sins. Theirs was a relationship and not just a religion. Their Lord was not dead nor a mortal like

71   Justo L. González, *The Story of Christianity, Vol. 1: The Early Church to the Reformation*, revised and updated (New York: HarperOne, 2010), 22-58; see also "Persecution in the Early Church: Did you Know?" *Christian History & Biography*, http://www.christianity-today.com/ch/1990/issue27/2705.html (accessed January 24, 2014).

the emperor. He was the living God, living in them in the person of the Holy Spirit. This reality demanded absolute loyalty even unto death. This living and loving relationship is reflected in the final words of Polycarp, the martyred bishop of Smyrna, who said when told to renounce Jesus, "Eighty and six years have I served him, and he never once wronged me; how then shall I blaspheme my King, who hath saved me."[72]

2. They lived and practiced a counter-cultural ethic and morality. The pagan Roman Empire was rife with immoral and abusive practices. Temple prostitution was the norm. Unwanted children, and especially girls, were "exposed" to the elements and left to die; those who were rescued were often reared for a life of prostitution.[73] Homosexuality was honored among the Romans. Women were treated as property and adultery was common. The poor, the sick, widows, and orphans were left to fend for themselves. In contrast, Christ followers were instructed to not love and be like the world. Jesus told his disciples to move beyond the legalism of the Pharisees. *You have heard that it was said . . . but I tell you* (Matt. 5:21 HCSB). Paul told the Roman believers to *not conform to the pattern of this world* (Rom. 12:2 NIV). John wrote, *Do not love the world or anything in the world* (1 John 2:15 NIV). To the contrary, they were to love God and their neighbor as themselves (Matt. 22:37-40). They were to live among the pagans in such a way that these would see their *good deeds and glorify God* (1 Pet. 2:12 NIV). In essence, their lives should be full of good deeds and

---

72   *Fox's Book of Martyrs*, ed. William Byron Forbush (Grand Rapids: Zondervan, 1967), 9.

73   Latourette, 124.

be such salt and light that the world would see Jesus in them, even when suffering, and ask *the reason for the hope* they have (1 Pet. 3:15 NIV).

According to historical observers, early Christians consistently demonstrated the call to love God and others and not the things of the world in practical and visible ways. Pagan writers observed that the early Christians did not expose their children and often rescued abandoned children. They cared for the sick, widows, and orphans. They looked after those in prison, particularly their fellow Christians. Even converted slaves were treated as equals in Christ, with freeborn and slave often being martyred together.[74] Perhaps most notably, once converted they abandoned the immoral practices of their past and faithfully loved their spouses and children, even under the worst duress and persecution.

3. They brought about change from the margins to the center. Being a marginalized church did not mean early Christians were not in influential or powerful positions. Scripture testifies of influential and wealthy Christians. Crispus (Acts 18:8) had been a synagogue ruler; Erastus (Rom. 16:23) was a city leader in Corinth; Aristobulus (Rom. 16:10) may have been a grandson of Herod the Great; Zenas (Titus 3:13) was a lawyer; Philemon was a slave owner. By the end of the first century, "Christianity was no longer confined to the lower strata of the Roman population . . . and was beginning to infiltrate into the most noble families, even into the imperial family itself."[75] The faith, therefore, spread geographically *and* into all the empire's

---

74   Bruce, 189-91.
75   Ibid., 164.

social, cultural, and economic groupings. This was not due to any organized strategy or methodology but to the compelling truth of the gospel.

Being a marginalized church also did not mean their only witness was their godly lifestyle. Those in the margins also spoke to those in the center. The gospel was certainly preached, but it was also defended and explained. During the second century, for example, erudite apologists produced volumes defending Christians from false accusations and arguing for the reasonableness of the faith.[76] Scholars, lawyers, educated bishops, nobility, and even those in royalty believed, preached, and lived out the gospel of Jesus. The move or spread of the gospel however, was from the margins of society to the center of position, influence, and power. From its beginnings in Jerusalem, through Antioch, into Asia, Macedonia, and on to Rome, the church was primarily a marginalized and often persecuted movement. Only those committed to the exclusivity of the Lordship of Jesus Christ were willing and able to withstand the trials and tribulations that accompanied such faith. Their verbal and lifestyle witness, guided and empowered by the Holy Spirit, turned the world upside down from margins to the center. What would it be like, however, when the church itself became the center?

The Church at the Center; Churches at the Margins

After three centuries of persecution and existing "on the periphery of social and political norms," Constantine's actions towards Christianity changed western history. From the margins of society, the church moved to the centers of power where it aligned with the empire. Driven by politics, the emperor manipulated

---

76   David J. Bosch, *Transforming Mission: Paradigm Shifts in Theology of Mission* (Maryknoll, NY: Orbis Books, 1991), 212, notes that "[t]ough-reasoned argument was necessary, for Christians had to understand their faith in a pluralistic world."

bishops and councils. He worked with the church to confront pagans and suppress heresy by force. Sword and cross were merged. The missions of empire and Christ became one. The western empire *was* Christian, like it or not.[77]

From one perspective, the church had triumphed. It appeared that the kingdom of God had come on earth. All that remained was to protect the kingdom from attacks by heretics or pagans. Although much good could come from this marriage of church and state, conflict and corruption was common. History tells of territorial wars between "Christian" states and kings and financial corruption and moral depravity. It records the justification of wars, slavery, and genocide under the supposed authority of Christ. The merging of the church and state at the centers of power also led to the Crusades. These dealt a permanent blow to the unity of eastern and western Christianity. They wounded relations with Muslims and established "a permanent image of brutal, militant Christianity" that still alienates much of mankind.[78]

For centuries the church was at the center. Only pagans and heretics existed at the margins. To a degree, this was true. Heresy has always been a challenge for the church. Pagans have always been in the world, waiting for the church to fulfill its missionary mandate. The problem for so many centuries was how these were dealt with, which was often through persecution, extermination or conversion by force. To exist at the margins of Christendom was dangerous and often lethal.[79]

---

77   David W. Shenk, "Three Journeys: Jesus – Constantine – Muhammad,"ed. Keith E. Eitel, *Missions in Contexts of Violence,* Evangelical Missiological Society Series, Number 15 (Pasadena, CA: William Carey Library, 2008), 7-8. Pocock et al, 103, notes that "Constantinianism involved the shift of the church from a minority to a majority status. Whenever Christian faith became an official or established ideology, the lordship of Jesus was compromised. Power rather than servanthood was glorified."

78   Winter, 150.

79   Bosch, 230, says that by the time of the "high Middle Ages – the structure of human society was finally and permanently ordered and nobody was to tamper with it. Within the divinely constituted and sanctioned order of reality, different social

The Protestant Reformation only solved part of the western Christendom problem. Dominant Roman Catholic views on Scripture, soteriology, and ecclesiology were challenged and changed. The prevailing notion of cultural and political Christendom, however, did not. State and church still existed in a symbiotic relationship. To be a citizen of the realm was to be a Christian, either Catholic or Protestant. In Protestant lands, power was not as absolute or centralized as it had been in Holy Roman Empire days, but the state and church still depended on each other for legitimacy. They were still sharing the center.

Historically, therefore, when the church was at the center, the margins were reserved for pagans, heretics, schismatics, and a growing number of non-conformists. Some examples include:

The Donatists: Controversy with the Donatists was one Constantine inherited from earlier persecution. This rigorist group insisted on "the empirical holiness of the church."[80] They measured holiness in terms of one's response to earlier persecutions. They denied the authority of any bishop who had been consecrated by those bishops who had under duress turned over copies of Scripture to persecutors. Although the group continued in existence for a couple of centuries, they were such a threat to the empire's unity that Constantine ruled against them in AD 316 and threatened them with banishment.

Dissenters of the Middle Ages: Numerous dissenting groups rose in opposition to Christendom's (Roman Catholic during this era) monopoly on belief and practice. Some were outright heretical, some had peculiar teachings, and some were groups seeking a return to New Testament teachings. The Bogomiles, Paulicians, Cathari (Albingenses), Petrobrusians,

---

classes were to keep their places. God willed serfs to be serfs and lords to be lords . . . All sensible persons were Catholic Christians, and the monopoly of the church, also as regards secular affairs, was undisputed. No 'pagan' groups remained in Europe, although there were, here and there, isolated pockets of 'heretics' or 'schismatics.'"
80   Justo L. Gonzalez, *A History of Christian Thought, Vol. II, From Augustine to the Eve of the Reformation* (Nashville: Abingdon Press, 1971), 28.

and Henricians all drew the ire of the religious center. It was "in opposition to the Cathari that the Inquisition arose."[81] The problem in analyzing these groups, notes historian Robert Baker, is the "sparsity of historical material." Most of what we know about these dissenters was written by their opponents, who held the centers of power. Still, in some cases, for example the Petrobrusians, "the evangelical nature of the things these men taught is evident." Their beliefs were characterized by a rejection of traditional dogma and a return to the Scriptures alone as authoritative teacher.[82]

The Waldensians: An important group to consider is the one named after their leader, Peter Waldo. Severely persecuted but surviving to this day, the Waldensians are often used as the example of the most evangelical of all dissenting groups during the Middle Ages. Cannon calls them "New Testament purists," who wanted to "purify Catholicism by simplifying it." Of course, this was interpreted by the Roman Catholic Church to mean its "destruction."[83]

John Wycliff and John Hus: During the fourteenth century, these two men were persecuted and, in Hus's case, burned at the stake. The Englishman, Wycliffe, helped translate the Bible into English and used its final authority to attack the "Roman Catholic sacramental system." In Bohemia, Hus repeated Wycliffe's teachings, preached against papal abuses and insisted on reform.[84]

The Anabaptists: During the sixteenth century, many radical reformist groups were lumped together as the Anabaptists. Many arose independently, but their common conviction was "that the presence of the Spirit of God in the lives of believers

81   William R. Cannon, *History of Christianity in the Middle Ages* (Nashville: Abingdon Press, 1960), 209.
82   Robert A. Baker, *A Summary of Christian History* (Nashville: Broadman Press, 1959), 178-79.
83   Cannon, 222.
84   Baker, 162-63.

called for a drastic return to the church as it existed in the New Testament period." Sharp disagreements arose about what exactly that meant and how it was to be accomplished. Some groups pursued a return through peaceful means. Others were extremists and fell into violence and the "establishment of the kingdom by physical force if necessary."[85] Whatever their doctrinal position or strategy, the Anabaptists were persecuted by "Roman Catholics and Protestants alike."[86] Regardless of who owned the center at this time, Christianity at the margins was not to be tolerated.

The Huguenots: In sixteenth century France, the Calvinist Huguenots were alternately persecuted and tolerated, and finally ruled against by Louis XIV, who "insisted on one faith, one king, one land."[87] Over 250,000 Huguenots fled France in order to escape vicious persecution by the established Roman Catholic Church.

Seventeenth Century England: Church history in England is the story of groups trading intolerance and persecution, and groups either seeking to purify the Church of England or separate from her. In 1660, the Church of England found itself once again the official church after a period of Presbyterian rule. In that year, persecution began against all forms of dissenters. Through a variety of official acts, dissenters were barred from participating in governments. Ministers were obligated to use the Book of Common Prayer in worship services, forbidden to conduct religious meetings, and often barred from even going to the cities where they ministered. Many laws targeted specific groups, but "all of them brought great trial to Presbyterians, Congregationalists, Baptists, Quakers, and Roman Catholics."[88]

---

85   John Dillenberger and Claude Welch, *Protestant Christianity: Interpreted Through its Development* (New York: Charles Scribner's Sons, 1954), 58-59.
86   Baker, 229.
87   Dillenberger and Welch, 88.
88   Baker, 290-91.

Baptists in England and Early America: The persecution in England during the sixteenth century touched all dissenting groups. However, Baptist historian Leon McBeth notes that after 1660, "Baptists were singled out for special abuse." They had been the ones "most vocal in advocating religious liberty" and had participated in the overthrow of the king and of the Church of England. Consequently, Baptists became to "some extent . . . the scapegoat for all the problems of church and state since 1640."[89] In colonial America, persecution varied. In the south where the Anglican Church was established by law, dissenter groups were restricted, particularly in Virginia. As the American Revolution approached and the Anglican Church found itself on the defensive, it got worse for Baptists. Their aggressive nature, their disdain for the state church, and their subsequent rapid growth led to Baptists being "whipped, fined, beaten by mobs, jailed, and/or exiled in an attempt to control them."[90]

Evangelicals in Latin America: The "indissoluble union of the altar and the throne" was nowhere more apparent than in the Spanish colonies of Latin America. They supported each other completely – the church defending the divine rights of kings and the king "upholding the authority of the Roman Catholic Church." Although the church was under the control of the crown (more so than any European country), it had freedom to control doctrine and implement religious discipline. The Inquisition was active in Latin America against "contamination from heretics, Jews, and Moslems." The result was that there were "few Protestant heretics in the colonies," and most of these were corsairs and merchants.[91]

---

89   H. Leon McBeth, *The Baptist Heritage: Four Centuries of Baptist Witness* (Nashville: Broadman Press, 1987), 113.

90   Ibid., 269-70.

91   C. H. Haring, *The Spanish Empire in America* (New York: Harcourt, Brace & World, 1963), 166-89 passim.

By the time Latin American countries won their independence from Spain and Portugal in the nineteenth century,
Protestants (or evangelicals) had gained a foothold in most
countries. Persecution, official or unofficial, continued well into
the twentieth century. Accusations against these marginalized
groups went from being agents of communism to agents of
North American imperialism.[92] Today the situation varies from
country to country. Suffice it to say that, although evangelicals
are still the minority in most countries, in many cases they are
far less marginalized than in previous years. Their continued
marginalization in countries like Uruguay and Chile, however,
is not so much by the Roman Catholic church as it is by growing
secularism, just as it is in Europe and North America.

Wherever these particular marginalized groups may have
been along the orthodox/heresy scale, during the height of
Christendom any opposition to church or state meant persecution or marginalization. The marriage of the powers at the center
meant mutual protection of interests. Although the doctrine
and practices of these marginalized groups vary dramatically,
what are the lessons to be learned from their history?

1. Taking a position at variance with the dominant religious, cultural, and political position is dangerous.
   Whether ridiculed, criticized, ostracized, marginalized, persecuted, or even exterminated, the center of
   religious and political power, and particularly when
   united in self-preservation, cannot be challenged.

2. Holding to biblical truth, truth which may not be
   recognized until later in history, does not exempt one
   from the wrath of the center. In fact, biblical truth is
   often the very reason persecution is so intense.

---

92   Samuel Escobar, *La Fe Evangélica y las Teologías de la Liberación* (El Paso: Casa
Bautista de Publicaciones, 1987), 111.

3. However the truth they held may be judged, these non-conformist groups took their positions seriously enough to die for them.

4. With some significant exceptions, most non-conformist groups believed the truth would win out on its own merit *apart* from political machinations and violent means.

5. Understanding and eventual vindication may not come until much later in history, if ever, this side of heaven.

During the centuries following the Reformation, things began to change. It was only as Christendom began to collapse that marginalized Christianity began the move to the center. Thus, the American experiment.

From the Margins to the Center of Influence

It can be argued that the most important element of the American experiment was religious freedom, something never before seen in human history. Without a doubt, we are still trying to work out the implications of the "free exercise" and "no establishment" clauses in our constitution. Nevertheless, with the coming together of a Reformation-modified Christendom, Enlightenment values, and the desire for freedom for all, the stage was set for marginalized Christianity to move to the center of influence. This meant that:

1. Whether or not the United States was founded as a Christian nation, the dominant, religious-cultural milieu was steeped in Judeo-Christian history and ethics.

2. The declared intention of religious freedom did not end continuing decades of established churches in some states. America has struggled continuously

to understand the application of religious freedom, especially as it applied to non-Protestants. Did it apply also to Jews? What about the huge numbers of immigrants from Roman Catholic countries? Could Native Americans practice their indigenous religions? What about the influx of non-Christian and even anti-Christian religions?

3. Religious groups which had been marginalized in the colonies, such as Baptists and Methodists, were able to grow. Without minimizing the role of the Holy Spirit or the evangelistic zeal of Baptists, Methodists, and others, the sociological, cultural, and political factors of the new independent country were in their favor.

4. New religious groups could spring up and prosper. Mormons, Pentecostals, Churches of Christ, Seventh Day Adventists, and others began and grew in a religiously free environment.

5. The freedom to worship, evangelize, move around the country, and influence the culture led to the informal establishment of Christianity – but mostly in its *civil religious* form – as America's religion. Protestantism in general and what we now refer to as evangelicalism in particular (which has historically been on the margins) had moved to the center of cultural influence, especially in the South and the Midwest.

Ironically, the informal establishment of Christianity, and particularly evangelical Christianity, was most noticeable in the last quarter of the twentieth century. Whereas Christianity was the assumed status of the country for generations, by the sixties it became clear that secularism was winning. Many Christians felt that both morality and religious freedom were being threatened. A significant response came when the so-called Christian Right mobilized to "take the country back" and rescue it from its continuing slide into secularism. The argument of this group, who represented some but not all evangelicals, was that America was founded to be a Christian nation, she had slipped further and further into secularism, and she needed to be returned to the state God and the founders intended. The quickest way to achieve that return was through the election of Christian officials, influencing politicians and the political process, and getting out the evangelical vote, particularly on issues of moral values and family concerns.

The Religious Right had a modicum of success; however, the reality is that success is hard to measure. It is impossible to know how the culture would have changed had there *not* been a voice speaking for pro-life issues, for example. Although the goals of the Religious Right have not been fully realized, it is recognized by the political establishment (the Republican Party in particular) that the influence of the evangelical vote and of evangelical leaders are to be recognized and heeded . . . for now.

How should the two-hundred-year informal establishment of Christianity be viewed? What did the "Christianization" of America really do? Some considerations include:

Cultural Christianity (civil religion). Although many Christians hope and fight for the establishment of a Christian culture, the inevitable result – proven throughout history – is cultural Christianity. On the positive side, the culture is shaped and directed by some sense of a Christian ethic and morality. On the other hand, Christianity is seen as a national or natural status for all citizens who chose to live a "good Christian life" rather than a new life resulting from repentance and faith in Jesus Christ and his atoning work. Ironically, evangelicals who insist on a personal experience of salvation by grace through faith are often the same ones arguing for a return to a nebulous civil or cultural Christianity.

Compromise. The result of cultural Christianity is that the gospel and the culture become so identified as to be indistinguishable. There are, indeed, surface aspects of the culture some choose to reject (smoking, dancing, drinking, and so on), but deeper core values which may contradict biblical principles are rarely examined.

Political marriages. In order to protect cultural Christianity, a marriage of necessity takes place with the political powers. This leads to the temptations that come with such a marriage: power, influence, money, and believing that the end justifies the means. It also leads to disappointments. Although some argue that the Republican Party is far closer to biblical morality than the Democratic Party, evangelical Christians are discovering that Republican candidates simply want to get elected. They, too, are susceptible to temptations and may water down the gospel to the lowest common denominator for political purposes.

Narrow focus. In the attempt to recapture the culture, evangelicals targeted only a few serious social issues, in particular abortion. The result was an inability or unwillingness to apply Scripture to the entire culture. Sure, we could speak against pornography, gambling, abortion on demand, and now gay marriage, but how often was the Christian Right willing to take on issues of poverty, racism, and the environment? Too often, those issues were only for left wing evangelicals.

From establishment to niche. Now that evangelicals have lost the center and are moving back to the margins, we have traded our cultural influence for a marketing niche. And, we have done this to ourselves more often than not. Evangelicals have become a group to court for the vote, to sell to, and to market to. The evangelical dollar is worth paying attention to.

The full evangelical gospel message? Not so much. We have built a self-imposed ghetto, useful for making a few extra bucks.

The African-American Church

Many groups which started on the margins stayed on the margins, for the American Experiment has obviously been an imperfect one, especially in regards to Native Americans and African Americans. The American Revolution left the great majority of approximately 400,000 black slaves in bondage, and "black Christianity stayed on the margin of American religious and civil life."[93] This marginalized church has much to teach the broader evangelical community as we all move closer to the margins of society and cultural influence.

Historically, groups were marginalized by doctrinal or practice issues. Some of these groups may have been ethnically identifiable, but the primary issue was theology. Most of the time black churches fit in with the dominant versions of Christianity with one major exception, and that was their opposition to the slavery narrative. The marginalization of the African-American church was not primarily theological, but due to the race of its adherents and their understanding of the biblical concept of freedom. In fact, whites had "enslaved Africans because of their reputed barbarism and lack of religion." Black Christians, however, "turned the formula completely upside down. White people were now the uncivilized pagans and Christianity was kept alive only by Africa's children." [94]

At first, many congregations in the late eighteenth century were "racially fluid." Whites grew fearful, however, that baptized slaves would desire freedom and more social benefits. They

---

93   Jon Sensbach, "Slaves to Intolerance: African American Christianity and Religious Freedom in Early America," *The First Prejudice: Religious Tolerance and Intolerance in Early America*, eds. Chris Beneke and Christopher S. Genda, (Philadelphia: University of Pennsylvania Press, 2011), 197.
94   Ibid.

thought too much biblical knowledge would lead to questioning the theological justification for slavery! Christianity for many slaves was a "creed of prophetic salvation, liberation, and even rebellion."[95] The result of white men's fear was that slaves were excluded from churches. So they left and successfully started their own congregations and denominations in both the north and the south. Opposition grew, forcing them to devise their own forms of worship, often in secret and hiding. In the bayous, in slaves' quarters, and in the backwoods of plantations, they developed the "invisible institution."[96] This marginalized existence among the "hush harbors" was considered conspiratorial and illegal by planters and could result in severe punishment.[97]

Even after slavery was abolished, prejudice in the north, Jim Crow segregation in the south, and a vast cultural gulf kept the African-American church at the margins of the dominant culture for the next one hundred years. While on the margins the church learned to be not only the religious, but also the social, cultural, and political center of the community. Pastors were not only church leaders but also community leaders. Eventually, by the mid-twentieth century, the Black church mobilized for justice and social action. It saw no dichotomy between the gospel of individual salvation and the political and cultural liberation of people.

The lessons to be learned from the African-American church include:

Freedom from abundance. Soong-Chan Rah notes that the white church is "familiar with a theology arising out of the context of abundance."[98] Listening to and learning from the

---

95   Ibid., 214-16.

96   C. Eric Lincoln and Lawrence H. Mamiya, *The Black Church in the African American Experience* (Durham and London: Duke University Press, 1990), 7.

97   Anne H. Pinn and Anthony B. Pinn, *Black Church History* (Minneapolis: Fortress Press, 2002), 12.

98   Soong-Chan Rah, *The Next Evangelicalism: Freeing the Church from Western Cultural Captivity* (Downer's Grove: IVP Books, 2009), 144.

African-American church (and other marginalized churches) can prepare the dominant evangelical church for life at the margins. The Black church has centuries of living at the margins in the midst of poverty and suffering. If our abundance disappears, Black church history could guide us. Unfortunately, as evangelicals become marginalized, many African-American groups have bought into the false prosperity gospel.

Perseverance. The African-American church is an example of perseverance in the midst of suffering.[99] Whether or not our future marginalization will include actual persecution, it will mean learning to live in the midst of severe criticism and ridicule.

Non-violence. A predisposition to non-violence should be the Christian norm, but history and current social media say otherwise. Injustice, oppression, and false accusations should be answered and addressed. The worst thing evangelicals could do, however, is to take up the sword. Our primary example is Jesus, who *when He was reviled, He did not revile in return; when He was suffering, He did not threaten* (1 Pet. 2:23 HCSB). At the same time, we can learn from a people who faced injustice primarily through non-violence.

Conclusion

When the church has been at the center of power and tied to the interests of the state, oppression and persecution of those who differ have followed. Many of these marginalized groups have been heretical. On the other hand, many have been reformist, sought a purer version of Christianity, or attempted to return to the authority of Scripture alone. For this, they were marginalized and worse.

The Reformation ameliorated that situation, but still left too much room for church and state coziness. The American Experiment, with both its secular and religious components,

---

99   Ibid., 158.

decentered Christianity officially if not culturally and unofficially. Broad evangelicalism, which existed at the margins, moved to the cultural, social, and political center. Thus, the status quo as a "Christian nation."

That status quo is changing with great speed. Evangelicalism will once again find itself on the margins of society. We must look at history, including aspects of our own American history, to understand what that means and how we are to live a marginalized existence. We also must look at Christianity as a minority status during the last century, for a marginalized existence has been the status quo of the church in most of the world.

Questions for Reflection and Discussion

1. What are some attitudes and actions that can be learned and applied from the persecution of early Christians?

2. What have you learned about having the church at the center of power? Are there possible advantages to this situation? Disadvantages?

3. What have you learned about heretical or schismatic groups?

4. What have been some benefits of a "Christian" America? What have been some negatives and dangers? Where do you think we are headed now? Why? What should be done about it?

5. What are some lessons we can learn from the experiences of the African-American church? Do these still apply today?

6. Should the church ever seek to be at the center and be the dominant controller of society? Why or why not?

Chapter 6

Learn from Global Christians

Christianity is not actually a western religion. Its ori-
gins lie in Palestine, and its future plies predominantly in
South America, Asia and Africa. . . . the numerical centre
of gravity of Christianity now lies in the developing world.
– Alister McGrath[100]

Indeed, it is said that more Christians have died as mar-
tyrs in the twentieth century than in all the period from the
beginning to 1900. The "Western" segment of the church
today lives in a bubble of historical illusion about the
meaning of discipleship and the gospel. We are dominated
by the essentially Enlightenment values that rule American
culture: pursuit of happiness, unrestricted freedom of
choice, disdain of authority. The prosperity gospels, the gos-
pels of liberation, and the comfortable sense of "what life is
all about" that fills the minds of most devout Christians in
our circles are the result. How different is the gritty realiza-
tion of James: "Friends of the world are enemies of God"
(James 4:4) and John, "If anyone loves the world, the love of
the Father is not in him" (2 John 2:15). – Dallas Willard[101]

We can learn much from the history of marginalized
Christians within a dominant Christendom environment and from those who have always been or suddenly found

---

100   Alister E. McGrath, *The Future of Christianity* (Oxford: Blackwell Publishers, 2002), x.
101   Dallas Willard, *The Divine Conspiracy* (San Francisco: San Francisco Harper, 1998), 214.

themselves in a minority, marginalized, and persecuted situation. Although evangelicals in the United States may never face the same degree of marginalization and persecution as these groups, we can still learn what community, witness, and having a prophetic voice should look like from the margins. As McGrath and others have noted, the demographics of global Christianity have shifted south.[102]

Life under the Dictators
The Soviet Union

The Soviet Union was the first state with an atheistic worldview bent on the complete elimination of religion. Its religion was no religion; it was ideologically opposed to all forms of what Karl Marx called the "opium of the people." In the first decades after the 1917 Revolution, persecution was concentrated on the Russian Orthodox Church, the dominant and officially recognized state church. At first, the evangelical groups (often lumped together and called Baptists) were the least endangered because most were from the working classes and were the least organized and hierarchical. Many had welcomed the revolution thinking it would alleviate the persecution they had faced under the previous Czarist-Orthodox marriage.[103]

In the 1920s and 30s, the Orthodox Church lost most of its clergy to labor camps or executions. Theological schools and publications were shut down. Property was confiscated, and marriage was detached from religion. All education was placed under state control, and by 1939, only 500 of the original 50,000 Orthodox churches were still open. Under Stalin, things got

---

102   "The twentieth century experienced the great shift of Christianity to the global South, a trend that will continue into the future. In 1970, 41.3% of all Christians were from Africa, Asia, or Latin America. By 2020, this figure is expected to be 64.7%." *Christianity in its Global Context:* Executive Summary June 2013, Center for the Study of Global Christianity, Gordon-Conwell Theological Seminary. It must be noted that this summary includes all branches and expressions of Christianity in its study.

103   James and Marti Hefley, *By Their Blood: Christian Martyrs of the Twentieth Century* (Grand Rapids: Baker Books, 1996), 226-233 passim.

worse for all groups, including Roman Catholics, Jews, and evangelicals. Things improved some under Stalin's successors, but most Christians had to remain cautious and participated in underground churches. In the final analysis, it is estimated that during the worst years of persecution, between 1917 and 1953, about sixty million Soviet citizens died as a result of communist policies. Sixty-six million were imprisoned, "of whom as many as half could have been Christian believers."[104] Similar stories and statistics were repeated in Soviet satellites and the Marxist countries of Eastern Europe.[105]

Nazi Germany

Nazi Germany was unique in that the Third Reich manipulated established Christianity for its evil purposes although it held a pagan and idolatrous worldview. National Socialism was aided by the established church in redefining Jesus and the Scriptures. First, the Old Testament was rejected for being too Jewish. Some Nazis argued it was "a cunning Jewish conspiracy" that threatened the German people. Second, Jesus was redefined to support their anti-Semitic agenda. Rather than being a Jew, he became a great Aryan hero and often portrayed as a "cruel anti-Semite." Jesus was appropriated by the Nazis for their racial, ethnic, political, and violent purposes. Third, the true church was not the body of Christ, but "the community of the *Volk.*"[106] This was simply "the ultimate in the identification of

---

104 Ibid., 264. See also Jack David Eller, *Cruel Creeds, Virtuous Violence: Religious Violence across Culture and History* (Amherst, NY: Prometheus Books, 2010), 194-5 and "Revelations from the Russian Archives: Anti-Religious Campaigns," *http://www.loc.gov/exhibits/archives/anti.html* (accessed 7 February 2014).1963), 166

105 Nik Ripken, *The Insanity of God: A True Story of Faith Resurrected* (Nashville: B&H Publishing, 2013) for stories of persecution in the former Soviet bloc countries.

106 Eric Metaxas, *Bonhoeffer: Pastor, Martyr, Prophet, Spy* (Nashville: Thomas Nelson, 2010), 166-68. Metaxas notes that Hitler was annoyed at Christianity not because it was nonsense, "but that it was nonsense that did not help him get ahead." Some of his key lieutenants, such as Martin Bormann and Heinrich Himmler, were passionately anti-Christian and wanted "the clergy crushed and churches abolished."

religion with culture." That is, Christianity *was* German history and German culture.[107]

In this context, the Confessing Church arose and separated itself from German Christians. In 1934, a group of pastors produced the Barmen Declaration, which repudiated the "bastardized theology" of the German Christians, opposed the anti-Semitism of the National Socialists, and emphasized the difference between Christianity and the German culture.[108] The end result was the imprisonment and/or execution of Confessing Church leaders such as Martin Neimöller, Dietrich Bonhoeffer, and many others. Most of these were also involved in conspiracies against Hitler, including plans for his assassination, which lent a political aspect to their arrest and imprisonment. However, their involvement in the conspiracy was driven by agonizingly thought-out implications of their theology. To oppose or kill Hitler was a way to serve God, who opposed such evil. In other words, to confess but not to resist was no better than to cooperate with criminals.[109]

China

The history of the Christian church in Communist China is one of the miracles and inspiring stories of the twentieth century. At the time of the Communist takeover, approximately a million Protestants and three million Catholics lived in

Evil though he may have been, Hitler was a shrewd politician who understood timing and how far he could go.

107 Joseph D. Bettis, "Barmen: What We Have Learned and What We Have Yet to Learn," ed. Hubert G. Locke, *The Church Confronts the Nazi: Barmen Then and Now*, Toronto Studies in Theology, Volume 16 (New York and Toronto: The Edwin Mellen Press, 1984), 176.

108 Metaxas, 222; Bettis, 177.

109 Metaxas, 360-612, quotes Bonhoeffer's best friend, Eberhard Bethge, as saying that the escalated "persecution of the Jews generated an increasingly intolerable situation, especially for Bonhoeffer himself. We now realized that mere confession, no matter how courageous, inescapably meant complicity with the murderers . . . we were approaching the borderline between confession and resistance; and if we did not cross this border, our confession was going to be no better than cooperation with the criminals."

China. Decades of persecution and purges followed. Because the country was isolated and communication was sparse, the assumption was that most Christians had been silenced, if not killed. After President Nixon's visit in 1972, China began to open its doors to the rest of the world ever so slightly. In time, it "became evident that millions of Christians had survived the Red purges." Although no one knows the exact number of Christians in China, the government approved Three-Self Movement has thousands of churches. The real story, however, is the fifty to more than a hundred million Christians worshiping in underground house churches. These have refused to bow to government expectations and restrictions and choose instead to worship in the underground movement.[110]

Currently, the status of the church in China is still precarious.[111] Although there is more freedom than in decades past, a renewed persecution of religion in general and Christianity in particular has arisen. In some cities, church buildings are being demolished and pastors are being arrested in an effort to control the rapid growth of unofficial Christianity.[112] The church has not faltered. Just as in previous periods of persecution, rapid growth is occurring in spite of persecution. Persecution serves as a "winnowing effect," separating committed disciples from Sunday Christians. True Christianity and legitimate congregations

---

110   Hefley, 76-78. The latest estimate from Asia Harvest is 105 million Christians, *http://asiaharvest.org/how-many-christians-china-1/* (accessed 12 July 2014). It should be noted that the Chinese Communists, like the Soviets, were ideologically opposed to any religion. Consequently, Muslims and Buddhists were also persecuted, the latter especially so in Tibet. Currently, the new religion of Falun Gong is severely repressed. See Eller, 195-7.

111   See Ripken, pp. 201-64.

112   According to the Pew Research Center the destruction of religious property is a global issue. In 2012 damage to religious property occurred in 34 countries, with the worst in Russia, China, and Tajikistan, Peter Henne, "A Look at the Damage Governments Inflict on Religious Property," *http://www.pewresearch.org/fact-tank/2014/07/10/a-look-at-the-damage-governments-inflict-on-religious-property/* (accessed 10 July 2014). See also, Brice Pedroletti, "China's Christians fear new persecution after latest wave of church demolitions." *http://www.theguardian.com/world/2014/jul/05/china-christianity-wenzhou-zhejiang-churches* (accessed 10 July 2014).

continue to be affirmed whether or not they are connected to visible buildings.[113]

Cuba

When Castro overthrew the dictator Batista in 1959, he was supported by many evangelicals. These had hoped for better conditions under Castro, who had stated that he was not a Communist and did not intend to set up a Marxist state. In 1961, he changed his tune, resulting in an atheistic educational curriculum, the control of churches, restrictions on assembly, obligatory registration, and the arrest of many Christian pastors and leaders. The Communist government thought that by arresting the leadership of local churches the church would wither up and die. The non-hierarchical polity in most evangelical churches simply meant that lay people stepped up to take leadership. The body of Christ not only survived, but thrived. Persecution drove believers to unity.[114]

In 1991, the Cuban constitution was changed and some religious restrictions were lifted. Religion was not to be discriminated against, and believers were allowed limited freedom. Growth continued, but when church buildings were full, the government was reluctant to grant permission to build more. Officials told Christians to "open your homes" and meet there.[115] This resulted in a church planting movement over the last few decades. Thousands of churches have been planted, and tens of thousands have come to faith in Christ. These "casa cultos" experienced exponential growth, partly as a result of government restrictions. Persecution drove church leaders to look past

113 Michael Gryboski, "Panel Looks at Christianity's Rapid Growth in China Despite Persecution," *http://www.christianpost.com/news/panel-looks-at-christianitys-rapid-growth-in-china-despite-persecution-120850/#!.* (accessed 4 June 2014).
114 Kurt Urbanek, *Cuba's Great Awakening: Church Planting Movement in Cuba* (Church Starting Network, n.d.), 68-77.
115 Will Stuart, "One sacred effort: an awakening in Cuba 'a powerful influence for Christ,'" *Commission Stories*, Volume 6, No.2 (IMB, Summer 2014).

church buildings and develop and train leaders for the house churches being started.[116]

Islamic Countries

Although Christians have been a minority in Muslim countries for centuries, at one time Christians comprised a significant number and influence in the Arab world. At the beginning of the twentieth century, Arab Christians (of many traditions) represented twenty percent of the population. In fact, "they had an outsize social footprint" in that they ran the majority of schools, hospitals, and other social services. They played a major role in the pan-Arab nationalist movement. Unfortunately, that situation has changed. Due to low birth rates, emigration, armed conflicts, political and economic stagnation, radicalization in Islam and subsequent persecution, Christianity has shrunk to no more than five percent of the population.[117]

The situation varies in Muslim countries. In Saudi Arabia, all faiths other than Islam are banned. In Indonesia, the world's most populous Muslim country, treatment of Christians varies in the different areas. An unintended consequence of America's invasion of Iraq has been the persecution of Christians, who had been left alone under Saddam Hussein. Hundreds of thousands have fled the country. The civil war in Syria has led to another war against the church. Christians are about ten percent of the population and have historically supported President Assad. He is a minority Alawite Muslim and has been sympathetic to other minorities. In Africa, the church suffers persecution in Sudan, Somalia, Nigeria, the Central African Republic, and elsewhere. Violence against Christians is increasing in Africa, led primarily by radical Muslims; there is "a strong drive to

---

116 Urbanek, 100.
117 Allen, 116-17.

purge Christianity from Somalia."[118] In Egypt, the ancient and well-established Coptic Church has long suffered oppression and persecution.

As in other times and contexts, persecution under Islam has not meant the end of the church. In Iran the church has grown under persecution. At the time of the Shah's overthrow in 1979, an estimated 220 Christians lived in Iran. In 2012 "the total had risen to 370,000."[119] Church planting movements have been reported in Bangladesh. Revival and rapid growth have also been reported in Algeria. Suffering in Uzbekistan has unified and strengthened different Christian groups.[120] Whatever the case may be in whatever country, the church of Jesus Christ will not only survive, but in many cases thrive under the worst of circumstances.

Lessons to be learned

The inspiring and convicting stories of persecution of the church around the world have filled numerous books. The previous summary does not do justice to our global brothers and sisters in Christ who have suffered, been imprisoned, and died for the name of their Lord. For those of us in the United States, what should we learn?

1. We must be more aware of the "global family of faith." As American Christians, we have the most freedom and wealth in the world. We may be, however, poor in understanding what it means to live as a disciple of Jesus in the worst of circumstances. We need to listen to the church in other countries when it comes

---

118   Tom Heneghan, "Reported Christian 'martyr' deaths double in 2013: report," *http://www.reuters.com/assets/print?aid=USBREA070PB20140108* (accessed 4 June 2014).

119   Allen, 130. Some have put the estimates as high as two million.

120   Anneta Vyssotskaia, "Uzbekistan: Church Learning to Overcome amidst Persecution." *http://www.worldevangelicals.org/commissions/rlc/rlc_article.htm?id=2408* (accessed 7 February 2014).

to matters of theology, politics, economics, and church life in a minority and marginalized context.[121]

2. We will have to learn what it means to live under real persecution and in real suffering. As American believers, we sometimes speak of persecution when we have only been slightly ridiculed. We speak of suffering when we have barely been wronged. The global church can teach us what it means to lose it all – freedom, material possessions, health, and even one's life for the sake of Christ. Do we know how to really count the cost? Do we really know everything is rubbish, loss, and filth when compared to knowing Christ Jesus? (Phil. 3:8).

3. We must examine what the essence of the gospel is, stripped of cultural baggage. That does not mean we strive for a cultureless gospel, for that is impossible and not desirable. It does mean we work at clarifying what is essential to the gospel and Christian life and what is preference, personal experience, or cultural packaging.

4. We must redefine success and faithfulness. We criticize the clichéd measures of success: "buildings, budgets, and bottoms in seats," but most of us still operate by those or similar measures. Somewhere in the margins, we must think of biblical faithfulness to doctrine, love of neighbor, obedience and witness, and the reproduction of disciples where success is slow, difficult, and hard to quantify.

---

121   Allen, 247. Allen, 249, also points out that in politics we will have to move beyond our categories of "liberal" and "conservative," for they are grounded in Western cultural understanding and don't always fit other cultures. In fact, the global church tends to be morally conservative and politically liberal.

5. We must finally learn how to have a prophetic voice while marginalized. When freedom of speech and assembly are limited, when cultural conventional wisdom says we are bigots and narrow minded, then how do we speak to culture? When access to the public square, academia, and popular culture is restricted or denied, how do we speak a prophetic word? We will have to learn a new way to say things, but even more important, a radical new way to live.

Take a biblical view of the sanctity of life, for example. In a society that continues to degrade and devalue life through abortion, pornography, violence, and the growing possibility of legal euthanasia and improved genetic engineering, how could a marginalized church speak to all these sanctity of life issues? What do we do if both political parties have compromised, when popular culture and conventional wisdom accepts abortion on demand, pornography, and the expression of violence as undeniable rights? What happens when medical ethics are driven by a pragmatic "we do it because we can" rather than by a biblical understanding of God's sovereignty over life? What do we do when all legal and legislative avenues have been exhausted?

We must do what the early Christians did in the Roman Empire, and as many already do: We provide alternatives to abortion and get in line first for adoptions. We express uncommon love and provide uncommon care for the aged, even if they are not our family. We have biological children without available genetic engineering, refusing to play God. We not only preach against pornography and violence, but we face up to our own lust for sex and violence and work hard at getting it out of our lives. We do all these things within a community of believers where accountability and encouragement are real. As a church, we must move beyond the modern ideal of the radically autonomous individual (even if Christian) whose religion and morality are "none of your business" to *confessing our sins to one another* (Jas. 5:16) and a genuine practice of Galatians 6:1-5.

For centuries, American Christianity has set the pace for success, resource development, and prosperity. That may not change any time soon; in all likelihood, we will continue to lead in material resources. As the center of global Christianity moves south, however, we may discover that we are far more like the Laodicean church of Revelation 3 than we realized. Would that we would learn from the global church how to trust and obey, how to be materially poor but rich in faith, and how to suffer and overcome!

Questions for Reflection and Discussion

1. What are some stories you have heard in the past about persecution around the world? How did you respond?

2. What knowledge do you have about current persecution around the world? Is this something discussed in your circle of friends? At church?

3. Do you think there is persecution in the United States? In what ways?

4. Are there any benefits or positives to living under persecution? What are they?

5. What do you think is the future of religious freedom in America? How should the church respond?

6. What can your church learn from the "global family of faith"?

7. Can you explain the gospel and the Christian life in a way that transcends culture? What are some possible

personal experiences or cultural baggage that may have influenced the way you understand the gospel in a negative way? If someone rejects your presentation of the gospel, is it the gospel they are rejecting or something else?

8. How do you define success in the Christian life? How does your church define success for itself? Do these definitions need some adjustments?

9. Think about the possibility of being in the margins of society when it comes to morality and ethics. What will you do when it is costly, painful, or dangerous to hold to the biblical understanding of sexuality, marriage, sanctity of life, or justice and peace? How could you and your church live out the biblical understanding of these in a culture that may reject you?

Chapter 7

Change Our Minds

It is my conviction, instead [of gaining political power]
that evangelicalism needs to rediscover the cross of Christ
and its fundamental challenge to the world. God chose to
redeem the world through an act that in the eyes of the
world was weakness and foolishness. At no point in the
narrative of redemption that centers on Jesus Christ is
secular power endorsed. Indeed, Jesus took every opportu-
nity to distance himself from possible political or secular-
izing interpretations of his ministry as Messiah.
– Alister McGrath[122]

Now here's the point I wish to make about the changing
church: We are the oddballs of our society! A Christian
with a biblical worldview and the desire to live out that
worldview is an outlier in America today. If we believe
and attempt to practice what followers of Christ have
always believed and practiced, then we are the weird ones
now. Orthodoxy is peculiar. We are not the majority. We
are very much out of step with the times.
– Robby Partain[123]

As American evangelical Christians, once we listen to and
learn from other believers what it means to live and min-
ister in a marginalized context, we must make some worldview

---

122   Alister McGrath, *Evangelicalism and the Future of Christianity* (Downers Grove:
InterVarsity Press, 1995), 170.
123   Robby Partain, "The Changing Church: *We are the Weird Ones Now*," Bluebonnet
Baptist Association Newsletter (February 2014).

adjustments. We must change our minds, our way of think-ing, our way of seeing and interpreting culture, and our way of responding to and living within a culture that has pushed us to the margins.

That the church is being marginalized is the assumption of many evangelical observers. To wit, Christianity in the United States is "very much on the periphery, for all its numerical strength;"[124] Christians are finding "themselves more and more on the margins in American society."[125] "We are no longer the moral majority. We are a prophetic minority."[126] The Christian "confessing body . . . is now no longer one of singular power and influence but that of a peripheral voice."[127] And on it goes from many others.

This real, current, and continued marginalization requires that we change our minds about what is happening to our sta-tus quo. That is the greatest challenge – to change our minds about our marginalization and see it as a potential blessing rather than a curse, because:

One, it will force us to exchange the idea of "culture con-version" for that of making true disciples of Jesus. The old Christendom model was to transform the culture by persuasion, legislation, or even by force to a Christian culture.[128] Christians should have an impact on the culture, including involvement in politics and legislation, but the biblical imperative is to make

124   Elesha Coffman, "6 Catholics, 3 Jews," *http://www.christianitytoday.com/ct/2010/mayweb-only/29-22.0.html?paging=off* (accessed 30 January 2014).

125   Ed Stetzer, "The State of the Church in America: Hint: It's Not Dying," *http://www.christianitytoday.com/ct/2010/mayweb-only/29-22.0.html?paging=off* (accessed 22 July 2014).

126   Naomi Schaefer Riley, "Russell Moore: From Moral Majority to 'Prophetic Minority,'" *http://www.christianitytoday.com/ct/2010/mayweb-only/29-22.0.html?paging=off* (accessed 22 July 2014).

127   Douglass John Hall, *The End of Christendom and the Future of Christianity*, Christian Mission and Modern Culture (Valley Forge: Trinity Press International, 1997), 2.

128   Craig Van Gelder, "Defining the Center – Finding the Boundaries," *Church Between Gospel & Culture*, eds. George R. Hunsberger and Craig Van Gelder (Grand Rapids: Wm. B. Eerdmans, 1996), 43.

disciples, not Christian societies. That is an exercise in futility and will only lead to disappointment.[129]

Two, biblical evangelism will be rediscovered and re-emphasized. Faith in Christ will no longer be about family tradition, social standing, the possibility of prosperity, or personal needs-meeting and personal fulfilment. It will be, rather, about denial of self and personal sacrifice, commitment, obedience, and possible suffering for the sake of Jesus.

Three, a marginalized church will cause us to find a political "third way." The traditional spectrum of left and right, liberal and conservative, will no longer be applicable to our status. We will have to work harder at thinking biblically and speaking theologically to all political parties and ideologies, for all fall short of a biblical worldview.

Finally, marginalization will challenge us to redefine ourselves as a community of believers. Once we no longer hold the cultural and political center and are more despised than respected by the majority of society, then we will need to define what we must believe, what we must be, and what we must do as the Body of Jesus Christ.

What we must believe
The Bible and Its Authority
What we believe about the Bible and how much we trust the authority of the Bible will be the line in the sand . . . but not so much between evangelicals and secularists as between evangelicals and liberal Christians. The future of all who claim to be Christians will be some degree of marginalization; however,

---

129 R. Alan Street, *Heaven on Earth: Experiencing the Kingdom of God in the Here and Now* (Eugene, OR: Harvest House Publishers, 2013), 243, insists that the "church is a signpost pointing to the kingdom. It does not expect to transform society into a paragon of Christian virtue any more than the British embassy in Moscow expects to persuade Russians to give up vodka and start drinking Earl Grey tea! When the church sees its mission as changing the culture of the country in which it resides, it will be disappointed."

those who hold to the supreme and final authority of an infallible Scripture *including* a biblical theology of life, sexuality, marriage, and morality will be the most marginalized. Secularists will be more than happy to point to progressive Christians and their interpretations as the norm. That liberal norm will be used to prove to society at large that evangelicals are intolerant, backward, and narrow minded.[130]

This appeal to the authority of Scripture does not mean that evangelicals will agree on all issues or have the corner on the market of interpretation and application. We have much to learn about understanding and applying what Scripture says about violence, poverty, creation, and injustice. This does not mean that we do not and will not continue to struggle with interpretation and application. That is part of our Christian journey.

This appeal to the authority of Scripture is not a denial of the sincerity or faith of those who hold a more liberal view of the Bible. It is an argument for starting with the assumption that Scripture is the infallible and objective norm, that fallen humanity's reason or experience cannot be fully trusted, and that the entire Bible applies to us today. This requires moving beyond chapter and verse proof-texting to the hard work of building a biblical theology that includes the entire Word of God.[131] We must believe the Bible is the supreme and sufficient authority for faith and practice in all situations.

---

130 Douglass John Hall, 22-23, who is not a conservative, says that he "would judge that the liberal and moderate denominations are characterized today by a palpable missiological confusion. The old liberalism with its enthusiasm for the ringing in of the divine Kingdom is now countered by a new liberalism that insists upon the rights of individuals to embrace whatever beliefs they choose." Furthermore, he notes, the "liberal temperament today can endorse foreign *aid* and global *service*, but not foreign *missions* and global *evangelism*; for the latter seems inseparable from white Western imperialism that liberal Christians, among others, have learned to regret and suspect." Hall does praise liberal and moderate churches for their fellowship (which he says is their only basis for existence) and their service to the community, but chides them for not making disciples and for not being able to give a reason for their hope.

131 For example, it is not helpful when addressing homosexuality to simply quote Lev. 18:22, true though it may be. Better is to explain a biblical theology of humanity,

Relevance of the Gospel

Having confidence in the authority of Scripture implies having confidence in its relevance for all people at all times. The Bible speaks today to every situation and issue. No, it is not a comprehensive history and science textbook, and there is no reason to take a naïve anti-science or anti-reason position.[132] No good reason exists to deny God's general revelation in creation. Good reason does exist, however, to carefully and consistently evaluate our understanding of general revelation by means of Scripture, as we depend on the Holy Spirit who inspired that Scripture and leads us in all understanding.

So, what is the relevance of the gospel for today? It is not simply a better way of life comprised of pithy religious sayings or legalistic rules to take note of and check off. Rather, God is on a mission to redeem his estranged creation through the person and work of Jesus Christ. He loves his creation – people and nature – and has had a plan from before the beginning of time to restore all things. He offers that redemption to all who repent and believe in Jesus Christ, receiving forgiveness of sin, new life, and the promise of eternal life. The cross of Christ is the means and the power for restoration of a relationship with God, with fellow human beings, and with his creation. This gospel of undeserved grace is relevant to every issue of contemporary life, including guilt, shame, addiction, injustice, and oppression. The gospel leads to a new way of life, but it is grounded in the acknowledgment of the seriousness of sin,

marriage, and sexuality using ample Old and New Testament passages. Conversely, to support homosexuality by simply saying that "Jesus never said anything about homosexuality" is also a form of proof-texting. For one, that statement betrays a denial of the authority of the entire Bible. Moreover, it is far better to look at all Jesus *did* say about marriage, sexuality, and God's original purposes that would definitely apply to homosexual behavior.

132 The Bible does, however, speak truthfully when it does address history and science. Still, reasonable, godly, and faithful interpreters will often disagree on specific interpretations. That fact does *not* diminish the authority of the Bible, but simply points to our fallen nature and lack of ability to perfectly and comprehensively understand God's mind and ways.

personal repentance, and trust in the exclusivity of the person and work of Jesus Christ on the cross. We must believe that the message spoken and lived out thousands of years ago is just as real and true today as it has always been.

What we must be

If we believe the gospel is true and relevant to all people and issues, then we must believe that God is actively in the reconciliation business and we are his kingdom ambassadors. Life on the margins does not mean retreat into ghettoized Christianity. It means learning to engage the culture as salt and light in a new way – from the margins rather than from the center of power and influence. This means we will have to be:

A Peculiar Community

We will have to rediscover the meaning of being *a peculiar people* (1 Pet. 2:9 KJV), which does not mean odd or strange. Modern translations do a better job of communicating the Greek by using phrases such as *a people for God's own possession* (NASB), *God's special possession* (NIV), and *a people for His possession* (HCSB). We are his, purchased by the death of his Son and now belong to him. We are members of God's kingdom and are agents of that kingdom – salt and light – especially from the margins. This *does* make us oddballs and a little strange, because we are living in a new and different culture called the church. We will no longer be a preferred group, a power block, or a group of movers and shakers. We will not even be the proverbial silent majority.

Understanding our new status will be important as we evangelize from the margins. We are not inviting people to simply accept a set of doctrinal beliefs or live their best life now, but to join "the world-changing kingdom of God,"[133] which has been and will be a dangerous and demanding place.

133 Rodney Clapp, *A Peculiar People: the church as culture in post-Christian society* (Downers Grove: InterVarsity Press, 1996), 167.

Ambassadors of Reconciliation

Being salt and light begins by being models of biblical grace, love, and forgiveness. This means taking sin *and* grace seriously. In the Bible, we find the clear definition of what offends God. We must then proclaim and demonstrate that God graciously provided the solution to sin. A voice from the margins, however, will require taking a hard look at ourselves first. How have we as evangelicals compromised with sin? We stand against abortion, pornography, and gay marriage, but what about materialism, consumerism, and a culture of violence and racism? Do we compromise in the name of patriotism? Have we pointed the finger at others' idols but failed to identify our own idols of success, pragmatism, and religious competition? A marginalized church will need to undergo pruning. What is believed and practiced will be examined and evaluated; those who are committed believers will be more obvious. Being a "cultural" Christian or weekend Christian will not be attractive anymore.[134] Once we have pointed the finger at ourselves, we can live and speak prophetically from the margins as a peculiar people of God, demonstrating the life of biblical grace that transcends all cultures and ideologies.

"The Least of These"

Gracious living requires the willingness to give everything up, to become like the least of these, to be last, and to be servants. All of this preaches so well – until we have to live it out. We like to talk about being a servant, but no one likes to be treated as one. No longer at the center of cultural and political power, a marginalized church will have no choice but to learn to model

---

134 Stetzer, "The State of the Church in America" notes the difference between cultural, congregational, and convictional Christians. The latter are the ones who will "count the cost." The others may eventually shed the label of Christian if the going gets too tough. For Stetzer, the "Church is not dying. It is just being more clearly defined." This is not, he says, "cause for despair," but rather "is a time to regroup and re-engage."

servanthood and sacrifice. This is how salt and light can be expressed prophetically. Can we love and serve those who have pushed us to the margins, who have taken away our rights, and who have determined to treat us as servants or worse? As the cliché says, "it is all about attitude." We must set aside the temptation to control, exercise power, be defensive, or offend and practice the humility of Philippians 2 not only with fellow believers, but toward the world.

What we must do

If we understand ourselves as a peculiar community, a new culture, models of grace, and having a prophetic yet marginalized voice, how then do we live?

Live as Disciples

This is not an argument for retreat from the world. Evangelicals and Bible-believing churches may be marginalized, but we must find new ways to engage the world. Christians need to seek ways to be engaged in the culture, whether in the arts, business, education, or politics. This engagement, however, will be more from a position of powerlessness than power and control. We do not seek withdrawal; we do seek to be salt and light wherever and however we come into contact with the culture at large. We speak, write, blog, and act, even when it may lead to ridicule, fines, or arrest. Our speech and behavior is not an effort to regain power and control or to legislate cultural conversion – that was the mistake of Christendom in all its expressions. To the contrary, we seek to love and serve in such a way that the world is drawn to Christ through our peculiar communities and our salty engagement with the world. Ironically, we are not seeking to transform the culture as much as we are presenting an alternative culture, the church of Jesus Christ. This means discipleship is not just for Sundays or in the Christian community and never simply personal or privatized. This discipleship is for every aspect of life, whatever the cost may be.

So how do we engage culture? To borrow a phrase from Justo Gonzáles, we must learn about "incarnate marginality." Gonzáles argues that the two primary historical Christian paradigms for cultural engagement have been either the Constantinian, in which the church was at the center of culture, power, and influence, or the Augustinian, in which the church saw itself as belonging to the City of God and regarded civil power as unimportant or part of the passing earthly city.[135]

The first paradigm can be seen in the Roman church, the Orthodox churches, and in most Protestant countries. It is also seen in Latin American Catholic countries and even in secular countries with official separation of church and state, for there is still a dominant religion or influential civil religion. The second paradigm is attractive to those who find they are not at the center of power, whether cultural, political, or economic. Many of the persecuted groups fit here, particularly the Albingensians, Anabaptists, and Latin American Protestants. González argues that the problem with both paradigms is they are both "triumphalist." The first is obviously so. The second becomes triumphalist because it places the church and believers at the center "by spiritualizing reality and convincing them that after all, the social and political reality is not all that important."[136] The church is at the center; it is just a different center, separate from the concerns of the world.

González makes an important point. The first paradigm is triumphalist by conquering culture and creation. The second is triumphalist by ignoring culture and creation and creating an alternative center. The first confuses culture and Christianity, so evangelism and discipleship are not necessary. The second

135 Justo L. González, *The Future of Church History* (St. Louis: Chalice Press, 2001), 151-52.
136 Ibid., 152-53.

retreats, builds a fortress, real or imaginary, and waits for eschatological rescue. The first compromises too much with culture and history. The second thinks it is above culture and history. Both are attractive to different Christians at different times, and we all tend one way or the other, sometimes alternating between paradigms. The idea of "incarnate marginality," which has a "measure of utopia," calls for disciples of Jesus to be not at the center, but at the margins. It is "the valley rather than the hilltop; it is the cross rather than the throne." Whether imposed on the church by circumstances, persecution, or simple overwhelming pluralism, believers will be more at the margins of culture and cultural power.[137] The response to this situation, whether from an underground church or a believer who is an elected official, is modeling the sacrifice and servanthood of Jesus. That counter-culture lifestyle, that new culture, will be the only thing that will turn the world upside down again.

Develop a Holistic and Servant Theology

Life from the margin will require a holistic biblical theology that will demonstrate sacrifice and servanthood. A clearly stated biblical theology will be necessary more than ever. The reality of sin, the need for repentance, and the power of the cross must be acknowledged. Biblical positions on life, sexuality, and marriage will need to be lovingly explained (and practiced) using all of Scripture. The margins will require evangelicals to tackle issues that have been driven by left or right ideological politics rather than biblical theology. They will need to address poverty, peace, justice, immigration, criminal justice, health care, and the environment. Without a doubt, many evangelicals do address these issues biblically, both in terms of immediate action and long term solutions. Unfortunately, we do so primarily from the perspective of the center with our own cultural, economic,

---

137   Ibid., 153-54.

and political leanings. Solutions from the margins look different. When we have given up most of our rights, positions, and possessions, we may see these issues from a new perspective.

Struggle with Evangelical Ecumenism

Life from the margins will also force us to re-examine what it means to be the church across denominational and traditional lines. Persecuted Christians around the world learn this quickly. What will evangelical ecumenism (perhaps cooperation is a better term for some) look like? We have experienced this kind of ecumenism as we have joined forces to stand against abortion on demand and gay marriage. Much, however, still divides us and some of it legitimately so. What are the primary non-negotiables we must agree upon? What are secondary and tertiary biblical interpretations and practices that we can agree to disagree on, yet join together as the Body of Christ? What really matters? Life at the margins will allow for neither doctrinal compromise nor dogmatic rules. Some denominational differences and distinctives may be important to maintain, but a marginalized church must work harder at finding the common ground that unifies us more than divides us. Our fruitfulness and faithfulness will depend on it.

Conclusion: Strangers in a Strange Land

The future of evangelicals in America will be different from what it has been in the past two hundred years. In many ways this change may be for the best. In other ways, it will be scary and dangerous. Whatever the future may hold, we will and should be living as "aliens and temporary residents," engaging the culture, loving people, and being salt and light (1 Pet. 2:11). We should not be surprised *when the fiery ordeal arises among you to test you . . . as if something unusual were happening to you* (1 Pet. 4:12). To the contrary, *that* life is historically and globally the normal Christian life.

Questions for Reflection and Discussion

1. What are some of the attitudes you encounter in people related to the condition of the church in America? Concerning our religious freedom? Concerning changes in the culture?

2. In a time when sin is not taken very seriously, what are some ways that your church can teach and explain the seriousness of sin? What are some ways to teach and explain the seriousness and the reality of grace?

3. How can we develop and maintain a biblical view toward our status in society, whether it is a preferred or a persecuted status?

4. How is your church "peculiar"? How are you different from the surrounding culture? In what ways are you too much alike?

5. What are some areas of your own life where you struggle to be a disciple of Jesus? What needs to be confessed and repented of? What do you need to do to surrender *all* to Jesus and his Lordship?

6. When push comes to shove and the church finds itself at the margins, how should she exist? What should our attitudes and actions be?

7. How do you see "evangelical ecumenism"? What are some ways your church can cooperate with churches of other denominations? Where should you draw the line and not join forces with them? What are the nonnegotiables in ecumenical cooperation?

Plan for Action – Part 2

The Authority Matrix

The bottom line is that we have a crisis of authority. That is, upon what basis will we continue to make faith and life decisions? This authority crisis is only going to intensify, especially as it relates to spiritual, moral, and ethical issues. Take a look at the following authority matrix and the accompanying questions:

More Objective		
Rationalism and Empiricism. "Truth" is to be discovered apart from revelation. Modern worldview; Science has the answers. The material world is ultimate. At best, Bible has ethical teachings.	Truth is revealed by God. Bible is authoritative and can be trusted. Authority is "external" – outside of humans. Timelessness of Biblical truth; applies to all humans at all times. Theology done in, by, and for the church.
Relativism. Postmodern worldview. Truth is constructed by community and experience. Truths are not to be imposed on others. Plethora of individual spiritualities. At best, Bible has a spirituality that is "true for you."	Scripture taken out of context. Hyperindividualistic interpretation. Legalistic and judgmental toward others. Focuses on "what it says to me;" non-historical approach. Scripture manipulated to fit felt needs.

More Subjective

Bible Least Authoritative — Bible Most Authoritative

1. How have you seen each quadrant expressed in contemporary Christianity?

2. How have you seen each quadrant expressed in other areas of society – school, work, media, pop culture, your own life?

3. How would you answer those coming from quadrants 1, 2, and 3?

4. Assuming that quadrant 4 is where we want to be (should be), how can you and your church:

    • Model and teach Biblical authority to your children? To your teens?

    • Learn to share the gospel to people in all quadrants, especially in 1 and 2?

    • Develop teaching and preaching that models and emphasizes Biblical authority?

Part III

Evaluating the Return

Chapter 8

Fear, Joy, and Trust

---

*Thus, I am arguing that in important ways quite like the
nation-state America, the church is a public, cultural, visible, political presence in the world. . . . [T]he culture wars
can be welcomed on the count that they help return us to
a place where we can conceive of Christianity as a way of
life, as a specific manner of being and doing in the world.*
– Rodney Clapp[138]

*After they called in the apostles and had them flogged,
they ordered them not to speak in the name of Jesus and
released them. Then they went out from the presence of
the Sanhedrin, rejoicing that they were counted worthy to
be dishonored on behalf of the name.*
– Acts 5:40-41 HCSB

The return of the church to the margins of society gener-
ates all kinds of emotional reactions. Some get angry
and defensive and want to oppose, and even fight against the
return. There are some legitimate reasons to push back, including issues of constitutional freedom. Others succumb to an
eschatological surrender, declare that the end times are finally
here, and wait for the rapture. Still others want to retreat into
a Christian fortress or ghetto, something quite tempting on
the worst of days! Others encourage the church to take a hard
look at itself and the changing culture, and try to create new

---

138   Clapp, 56, 75.

ways to proclaim the gospel and be salt and light. Some issues to consider include:

Reasons to Fear
Loss of (some) Freedom

The reality is that we will lose some of the freedoms we have been accustomed to. Both modernity and post-modernity have encouraged the privatization of faith and religion. Modernity conceived of faith as a private concern of the autonomous individual, and post-modernity places the locus of pragmatic faith and truth in the individual's experience. The marginalization of the church implies less tolerance toward freedom of religion, when that religion is understood as faith directing and influencing every aspect of life, including public life. Freedom of religion is being redefined as freedom of worship only, understood as what one does in private or with a particular group on Sunday. Do what you will in "church," but keep it there. Don't impose any of your beliefs on society and culture (even through simple evangelism or apologetics).

We can debate what a legitimate freedom is and what may be loss of a traditional civil religion preference. The latter are usually noticed first and are often argued over. For example, raising a ruckus when a business uses "Happy Holidays" instead of "Merry Christmas." We will certainly not agree with secularists on religious freedom, and we often disagree among ourselves because cultural Christianity is so engrained in our consciousness. The reality is, however, that marginalization will lead to limits on some of our real religious freedoms.

Loss of (some) Influence
If we fear that we may lose some religious freedom, then we fear an even more significant loss of moral, cultural, and

political influence. The reality is that the church's influence must be understood in a different light. The big difference will be between influencing for a "Christianized" country, meaning mostly civil religion (generic prayers at public events, "In God we Trust" motto, the marketing of WWJD materials, etc.) and being a kingdom community of salt and light in the midst of a post-Christian and anti-Christian society. We will have to learn better how to pick our battles. Will we spend our time, energy, and resources trying to recapture "Christian America," or will we devote ourselves to learning how to live and act as the church has done historically and globally from the margins?

Loss of (some) Vision

The marginalized church must rediscover a biblical vision for itself. What are we about and what are we supposed to do? The two extremes to avoid are a recapture of Christianized civil religion and a retreat into a Christian ghetto. The challenge is to produce fruit while living at the margins. But how does an active, orthodox church survive on the margins and yet stay theologically healthy and missionally active? Churches on the margins seem to go one of three ways: One, some are tempted to be successful, to be accepted, and to move to the center of political and cultural influence. Two, some fade away into irrelevance or disappear under duress. Three, others morph into something unorthodox like the prosperity gospel or some other expression of cultural accommodation.[139] Rodney Clapp is correct when he argues that the church must see itself as a "new and unique culture" which exhibits a true community of love and service, practices the "peculiar politics" of forgiveness, and perpetuates itself through evangelism.[140] The new vision must

---

139 Thanks to Dr. Robby Partain for posing this question and suggesting the answers in an email dated 16 June 2014.
140 Clapp, 89-90.

be one of being on the margins, *staying* at the margins, and fruitfully living and ministering like Jesus from the margins.

Reasons to Rejoice

More than fear, a return to the margins has the potential for great blessing and benefit. It offers the church opportunities to rejoice as we rediscover God's work in us and through us.

Suffering for Christ's Sake

Few of us in the Western world, and even fewer in the United States, know what it is like to suffer for Jesus' sake. We suffer illness and death, poverty and oppression, mental stress and emotional distress, but these are generally due to the fallen state of creation and humanity. Bad things cause us to suffer, but they are usually not directly for Christ's sake. They are the lot of fallen humanity. Without a doubt, God permits and uses this suffering for a variety of reasons, and it can serve to both build our faith and strengthen our witness. Our suffering can glorify God and point others to Christ. It is part of our ongoing sanctification.

It is rare that one of us suffers directly for our faith in Christ. At worse, we may be ridiculed, ostracized, and criticized. We have yet to be systematically fined, fired from our jobs, passed over for promotions, or jailed because of our faith. Non-Mormons living in parts of Utah and Idaho will argue that they have been discriminated against due to their faith. At times throughout our history, Jews, Roman Catholics, and other groups have suffered discrimination in parts of the United States. As odious as these practices have been, they were not generally government sanctioned or applied across the country. Furthermore, they were practices by one religious group (usually based on a misunderstanding of biblical Christianity) against another religious group. What we are facing in the future is intolerance by secularists and a post-Christian society toward religion in general and Christians in particular.

Why is there a reason to rejoice? Although we may never suffer the persecution believers faced in the Soviet Union, or currently in China, North Korea, and Islamist countries, we are staring right at a Western European type of marginalization, and perhaps worse (although shame on us if we even think of comparing our marginalization with the persecution of our global family). Limitations on freedoms – and cultural, political, and economic marginalization – will be our new reality, such that we will no longer be able confuse biblical Christianity with American culture.

To rejoice in the face of suffering for one's faith is prevalent in the biblical witness. Many of the Old Testament saints *were stoned . . . were sawed in two . . . died by the sword* and were *destitute, afflicted, and mistreated* for their faith in God (Heb. 11:37). Jesus suffered on our behalf without complaining or fighting back (1 Pet. 2:21-23; 4:1). Consequently, we should and will suffer for who we are and what we do, something about which we can rejoice (1 Pet. 3:13-14, 17). Suffering – trials, tribulations, and persecutions – are guaranteed (Mk. 13:13; Phil. 1:29; 1 Pet. 4:12), but are temporary and productive (2 Cor. 4:17), character building (Jas. 1:3-4), shared with Jesus (1 Pet. 4:13), and worth rejoicing over (Acts 5:40-41; Rom. 5:3; 1 Pet. 4:13-14, 16). These passages and the reality of suffering throughout history led C. René Padilla to argue that the church must be characterized by suffering.[141] In other words, if the church is not suffering to some degree, is it really standing against the prevailing world system? We do not need to minimize the real pain we experience as fallen human beings in a fallen world. The reality is, however, that most of us in the West have had little reason or

---

141 C. René Padilla, "The Kingdom of God and the Church," *Theological Fraternity Bulletin* 1-2 (1976), 11-12.

opportunity to suffer for the name of Jesus. We should learn from the stories of our global brothers and sisters that God uses marginalization, oppression, and persecution to build faith, to provide an incontrovertible witness, and to prune his church.

Pruning and Holiness

The cliché states that when times get tough, the tough get going. The implication is that the not so tough quit, drop out, or wither away. This was the case for Jesus and some of his followers in John 6. In this passage Jesus calls himself the Bread of Life and teaches that the *one who eats this bread will live forever*. Some of his disciples complain the teaching is hard and *turned back and no longer accompanied him* (John 6:66). Later when threatened with the possibility of arrest, Peter denied Jesus three times, although he was gloriously restored. The apostle Paul notes that Demas deserted him *because he loved this present world* (2 Tim. 4:10), and John points out those *antichrists* who *went out from us, but they did not belong to us* (1 John 2:18-19).

The point is that the church has always experienced pruning brought on by difficulties, suffering, and persecution. Those who have counted the cost of following Jesus stick it out, even at the cost of their lives. As the church is marginalized, a pruning will take place. This does not mean some of us should stand in judgment of others and expel them from the fellowship. Those who in reality did not *belong to us* will leave on their own accord. In fact, those who *tasted the heavenly gift* but are not committed may fall away into isolation and fruitlessness (Heb. 6:4-6). The lines will be drawn, as Ed Stetzer puts it, between the "cultural," the "congregational," and the "convictional" Christians.[142] As

---

142 Stetzer, "The State of the Church in America," *Cultural Christians* believe they are Christians "because their culture tells them they are." *Congregational Christians* are similar to these, but have "some connection to congregational life." *Convictional Christians* "actually live according to their faith."

marginalization makes living the life of Jesus more demanding, many will show their true colors.

This pruning will lead to and demand a greater holiness, personal and corporate. This is not a call for a return to pharisaical legalism, where we are proud that we don't dance, drink, or smoke. It is a call to rediscover a holiness that defines and expresses being set apart for God. It manifests itself in loving relationships within the church and with serving attitudes and actions in the world. Pruning distinguishes the church not simply as "countercultural," which usually means "counter to a few negative aspects in my culture," but as a new culture led by the Spirit that is set apart by God for the purpose of reaching and blessing the nations. This new culture of holiness represents all aspects of the character of God and not a select few qualities that are easy to manage, measure, and check off.

Clapp speaks of this kind of lifestyle as "sanctified subversion." He gives biblical examples of those who lived within a corrupt system and managed to subvert it, direct it, and use it through their personal holiness. Joseph changed the direction of the Egyptian empire. Esther worked behind the scenes to save her people. Daniel and his friends judiciously and discreetly resisted. In fact, Jesus speaks of being *wise as serpents and innocent as doves* among the wolves of the world (Matt. 10:16).[143] He even praised those who used the system wisely (Luke 16:8). Pruning will therefore lead to a holiness that takes place *in* the system and even uses the system, but in a sanctified way.

Furthermore, this is a holiness that is motivated and driven by a Spirit-filled community that is both attractive to the world and incarnated in the world. Holiness like that of Jesus is filled with compassion and mercy for the least, the last, and the lost. It is personal holiness, but not solely personal because it

---

143   Clapp, 202-03.

is expressed within and from the church – the community of believers who are together at the margins.

Rediscovering Community

A struggle for many individualistic Americans is to see the church as more than a collection of like-minded (hopefully) individuals. The biblical concepts of church as family, body, temple, and flock were normal and easy to understand for those of Hebrew backgrounds. They are often radical and difficult to fully grasp in a culture that celebrates individualism, the lone wolf, and self-actualization. Some might argue that the healthy emphasis among evangelicals on the nuclear family (which is disintegrating and under attack) has had the unintended consequence of minimizing the New Testament teaching of the family of God. Jesus said he came to bring division in families, meaning that loyalty to him overrules biological and sociological loyalty (Luke 12:51-53). He pointed to his obedient followers as his true family (Matt. 12:46-50). The call to his disciples to follow him compelled James and John to leave their home, their business, and their father (Matt. 4:21-22).

This biblical emphasis on our new family does not diminish the importance of the biological family, in either its nuclear or extended expressions. The new family is an acknowledgement that biological families are made up of fallen people and often dysfunctional. The kind of loving community John describes, encourages, and commands in his first letter transcends biology and is possible only among those who are spiritually reborn and submissive to the will of the Holy Spirit. The church is not merely a gathering of individuals, but a family or body of people who have new life in Christ and have been baptized into a new existence, a new family, and a new community, which supersedes all biological family ties, as important as those are.

The marginalized church will need to rediscover what it

means to be this kind of family. This rediscovery will be both a necessity and an opportunity. It will be necessary, first, because we are made by God for community. Second, it will be necessary because we need each other for encouragement, support, and accountability while we live in a system that wants to declare us a nuisance and irrelevant. This opportunity allows us as a community to show the world what the kingdom of God is supposed to look like – like that seemingly unrealistic and impossible loving community as described by John in his first letter. We will learn to use the Sermon on the Mount as a "plebian political resistance guide"[144] and will have the opportunity to live and act in ways that reveal the bankruptcy, futility, emptiness, and corrupt politics of the world system(s) that oppose the kingdom of God.

Revival from the Margins

Evangelicals often pray for revival in America. Sometimes that prayer is linked to a return to Christian America, but that does not have to be the case. Revival, which may be defined several ways,[145] does not have to mean a return to the "way things were" in the past. It does, however, mean a work of God that leads to a return to God, whatever he may have in mind for the present and the future of America. Throughout history, revival in the church usually came at a time of spiritual decline and often first among the least influential in society – youth and college students, coal miners, and marginalized churches. A reason to rejoice, the good news, is that God may prune his church through marginalization, driving us to greater commitment,

---

144   Ibid., 203. Clapp is quoting Walter Wink.

145   Evangelism professor Alvin Reid says "revival or an awakening simply refers to a movement of God among His people, restoring them to their first love" and that "Revival refers to God's work among His people. True revival always leads to effective, passionate gospel-centered change." Alvin Reid, "Roar: The Deafening Thunder of Spiritual Awakening," *www.alvinreid.com/wp-content/uploads/roar.pdf* (accessed 14 August 2014).

stronger community, and more fruitfulness as an alternative culture. The bad news, however, is that pruning and revival may be God's preparation for even greater trials and persecutions. This is bad news only from one perspective, because it also means that God will be teaching us more about himself.[146]

Furthermore, when the evangelical church is shoved to the margins and loses its current power and influence, we will join others already at the margins. These are accustomed to powerlessness and may be ripe for use by God in revival. Frequent and recent reports of the beginnings of revival have surfaced among Native Americans in the United States and First Nations in Canada. Few people have been as marginalized as these have been over the last five hundred years. Much of the current growth among evangelical churches is among new immigrants to America, most of whom live at the margins of culture. Transition and change in family life, work, and culture are driving many to seek the Lord. Marginalized peoples and communities that have always felt powerless – poor neighborhoods, the border with Mexico, ethnic minorities, the incarcerated and their families – are the ground from which spiritual awakening can spring. The possibility of revival coming from existing or newly marginalized people is a reason to rejoice.

Hope and Revelation

The marginalization of the evangelical church in the coming decades is not necessarily reason for despair. God can and will use this new status in surprising ways. He chose *uneducated and untrained men* to confront and confound religious leaders (Acts. 4:13). He did not choose the wisdom of the world,

---

146 "An awakening may be God's means of preparing and strengthening His people for future challenges or trials," for "throughout history, renewal has often come before persecutions and severe trials that God sent to test and teach His people," "Patterns of Spiritual Renewal," *http://www.christianitytoday.com/global/printer.html?/ch/1989/issue23/2307.html* (accessed 14 August 2014).

but rather chose the world's insignificant and despised things to demonstrate his power (1 Cor. 1:28). The very cross was *a stumbling block to the Jews and foolishness to the Gentiles* (1 Cor. 1:23). Knowing this truth, we can rejoice and hope in what God can and will do in spite of and through the marginalization of the church.

Whatever one's interpretation of Revelation may be and whatever one's preferred eschatological scheme, the vision and promise of Revelation 5:9-10 gives hope that God can work through all these challenges in surprising ways. People from every tribe and language and nation, including those who have been and are marginalized, will one day stand redeemed before God. That the global south is now the church's center of gravity implies that marginalized people are the majority of these redeemed saints! The gospel is spreading throughout Latin America, Africa, China, parts of India, and in many closed countries. The powerless and the marginalized *are* the essence of the church.

In America, marginalization opens the door for the serious expression of kingdom community, for undeserved and unappreciated acts of service to the world, and for the great possibility of revival. Will we fear or will we rejoice? Will we fear or will we trust?

Reasons to Trust
The Mission of the Father
The marginalization of the evangelical church in America, however, whenever, and to whatever degree it takes place, is no obstacle to the completion of the mission of God. Our God is a missionary God on a mission to redeem his fallen creation. He chose Abraham and his descendants to be missionary light to the peoples on earth so that these may be blessed through Israel (Gen. 12:3; 26:4). Their calling, their very existence, and

their life in the Promised Land was so God's name would be proclaimed and known in all the earth (Ex. 9:16; Psalm 67:1-2). The nation of Israel was not chosen in and for itself, but as a particular means to accomplish God's universal goal of blessing all nations.[147]

Periodically Israel had to be reminded of this purpose – for example, through the prophet Jonah. When they failed to live up to their calling of loyalty and obedience to God, which was part of their witness to the nations, they suffered defeat and exile. None of their failure, however, kept God from fulfilling his promise of redemption. That promise culminated in the sending of the Son by the Father (John 3:16; 20:21). This Jesus Christ, God in the flesh, perfectly revealed, obeyed, and fulfilled the Father's mission. During any marginalization or persecution we may suffer, we can hold on to this truth: God's mission has been perfectly fulfilled in Jesus Christ (John 17:4-6). Whatever we may go through is simply part of being a witness and a blessing to others in the expression of his mission on earth. While on earth we will be hated, but protected. We have been sent into the world, so others may believe through us (John 17:14-15, 18, 20). We are in Christ, protected by Christ, and part of the Father's mission in the world as we wait for the return of Christ. We can trust because God is on a mission and we are privileged to be part of the fulfilment of that mission.

The Sacrifice of the Son

The Father's mission is to redeem his creation, and that climaxed at the cross through the sacrifice and resurrection of his Son. Jesus Christ died *for the ungodly*, and thereby we have been made righteous, reconciled to God, and saved from wrath (Rom. 5:6, 9-10). This new life means we have died to sin, been

---

147   Christopher J. H. Wright, *The Mission of God: Unlocking the Bible's Grand Narrative* (Downers Grove: InterVarsity Press, 2006), 222.

raised to a new way of life, and thus live with him both in this life and eternally (Rom. 6:1-2, 4, 8-11).

First, as disciples of Jesus we have trusted his completed work on the cross and become members of his kingdom. As potentially marginalized and persecuted disciples of Jesus, nothing changes. We believe that anything we could possible experience pales in light of his sacrifice for our sins. We trust, therefore, in his sacrifice, following his example *in order to live the remaining time in the flesh, no longer for human desires, but for God's will* sacrificing ourselves if we must (1 Pet. 4:2; 12-13 HCSB).

Second, as disciples of Jesus we trust in the reality and the power of his resurrection. God has raised Christ from the dead, a reality that guarantees our own resurrection at his second coming (Eph. 1:20; 1 Cor. 15:20-23). We now live "between the times" assured of his living presence in and among us in the person of the Holy Spirit (1 Cor. 6:19; Gal. 2:20), of his advocacy for us at the right hand of the Father (Eph. 1:20; 1 John 2:1), and of his ultimate victory over sin and death (1 Cor. 15:21, 26, 54-57). The reality of this hope does not call for withdrawal or passivity in this life, but rather it demands faith, action, commitment, doing the good works that have been prepared for us and standing firm in grace (Eph. 2:10; 2 Pet. 3:14, 18) even when marginalized by the world. This is how we know that in spite of marginalization or persecution, our *labor in the Lord is not in vain* (1 Cor. 15:58). As the song says, "Because he lives," we can face whatever the future may hold for the evangelicals in America.

The Presence of the Spirit

We trust in the midst of marginalization because we have the promise of the presence and the power of the Holy Spirit (John 15:26; 16:7-11). The Spirit teaches us (John 14:26), leads us to truth (16:13), guides us when under duress (Matt. 10:19-20), protects us (1 John 4:4), and empowers us to be witnesses and make disciples (Acts 1:8). Although it is probably difficult for most of Westerners to imagine it, the worst of circumstances reveals the presence and power of the Holy Spirit. Jesus experienced this reality to a depth we cannot imagine (Matt. 4:1). The apostles could stand up to opposition and persecution because they had been filled with the Spirit (Acts 2:4; 4:8). Paul knew firsthand how to depend on Christ's power in him (2 Cor. 11:23-27; 12:9-10). In a more contemporary setting, Nik Ripken tells story after story of believers who suffered terrible persecution in the days of Soviet communism, in present day China, and in Islamist countries. The testimonies of these leave no doubt of their complete dependence on the Holy Spirit through the worst persecution. They sang, they memorized Scripture, they witnessed. Ripken says "suffering believers" all over the world were "doing the very same things to survive, experiencing the presence of the very same God."[148]

Most American evangelicals can conceive of the power of the Holy Spirit only as the one who can make our day better, see us through a stressful situation at work, or empower us to do well under pressure. We obsess over how many gifts he has given us, which ones are valid for today, and what is the appropriate way for these to be expressed in the church. Now, these concerns are biblical and part of the life of the church. They are important, but we have little basis on which to speak of our dependence on the Spirit when we hear what our brothers and sisters in Christ are victoriously experiencing (not necessarily surviving) around the world. At that point, we will be able to rejoice in and trust the presence and power of the Holy Spirit as never before.

---

148 Ripken, 296.

Conclusion: And now for the good news

The story is told (and maybe embellished) of an American pastor visiting some of the underground churches in China. With all good intentions, the pastor tells a Chinese house church leader that churches in the United States are praying for persecution in China to stop. The Chinese pastor responds quickly, "Oh, no, please don't. We are praying for persecution to begin in America."

Nik Ripken also tells of a believer who suffered horribly at the hands of the Soviet communists. This saint begs Nik and all Americans to never "ever give up in freedom what we would never have given up in persecution!"[149] Unfortunately, we already have. We have bought into materialism and consumerism. We have confused Christianity with partisan politics and nationalism. We have made discipleship more about knowledge than about obedience. We have made Jesus into our own image, the church into our own possession, and truth into a personal commodity.

Perhaps some historical perspective is due. The world has always been a tough place to live – poverty, persecution, sickness, world wars, and natural disasters fill the history books. The United States has experienced civil war, world wars, epidemics, economic depressions, crime and violence, and moral degeneracy. I don't know that today is any worse than other times in our national history. We simply know more and report more of what is going on. It is certain, however, that we are facing serious and unique issues of morality and religious freedom. As bad as things may have been in the past, at least we could all appeal to a generally accepted standard even if we did not always follow it. Today any mention of an absolute authority, especially biblical authority, is rejected. At another

---

149   Ibid., 196.

time, we could have debated on an equal footing. Today, that equal footing is being intentionally eroded.

None of us wants to lose even a modicum of religious freedom in America. Although it is likely we will never reach the levels of tyranny found in other parts of the world, we will be pushed further and further to the margins of society. We will barely be tolerated, if at all, ridiculed, and treated as second-class citizens. In one sense, I do not look forward to it, but in another I can't think of anything better for us.

Marginalization is a reason to hope. We will be forced to examine our cultural Christianity, including all the ways we have confused the "American way of life" with biblical Christianity. We will be required to rethink and restate what it is we believe. We will need to cast off unbiblical definitions of faithfulness and success. We will have the opportunity to focus on what it means to do biblical evangelism, to make true disciples, to be the church, and to serve others who are powerless and marginalized. We will have the privilege to rediscover what it means to be the church – a peculiar community – that demonstrates to the world what it means to love each other. We will be compelled to love and serve those who despise and reject us in ways that will cause the world to look to the Father. We will be able to praise God for the opportunity to suffer for the sake of Jesus, knowing that he is Lord of Lords. Finally, we will come to understand that our new status is normal. We should not see it *as if something unusual were happening* (1 Pet. 4:12). It is an opportunity to know for certain that the *God of all grace, who called you to His eternal glory in Christ Jesus, will personally restore, establish, strengthen, and support you after you have suffered a little* (1 Pet. 5:10).

Questions for Reflection and Discussion

1. When you think about the way things are progressing in America, how do you feel? Why?

2. In what ways will the church have to rediscover a biblical vision for itself? What will the church have to do to prepare for life at the margins?

3. Are you prepared to suffer for Christ's sake? How? What must you do to get prepared? When you think of suffering for Christ's sake, what thoughts and feelings do you have?

4. How does the idea of "pruning" in the church set with you? Why?

5. What about personal holiness? What are some things – attitudes, behaviors, habits, dispositions, beliefs – in your life that need to change to better reflect the character of Jesus?

6. What about "corporate" holiness? What does your church need to change as a body – attitudes, behaviors, habits, traditions, methods, beliefs – to reflect the character of Jesus?

7. Think about the concept of "sanctified subversion." What does that mean to you? What could it look like where you live? What are some biblical ways to "subvert"? What are some possible misunderstandings and misapplications of that concept?

8. What are some ways your church could learn to be a more biblical body of believers? How can you *be* the church?

9. What are some ways your church can serve your

community, especially those who are most antagonistic to the church?

10. What are some ways you and your church could
take a stand for biblical morality and still show love
and compassion for those who disagree in word and
action? What do you do, and what will you do, when
they come to your church to join or to disrupt?

11. What are some things you and your church should
stop, start, divest of, or change to reflect being a kingdom disciple and community?

12. What are some ways your church can prepare for the
possible loss of some freedoms? For example, what will
you do if churches lose their property tax exemptions?
What if new zoning laws won't allow new construction of church facilities? What if it becomes illegal
to preach against homosexuality? What if charitable
contributions are no longer tax deductible? None of
these may come to pass; however, if they do, do we have
some kind of response other than an angry political
one (although that may be necessary)?

13. What is the most radical thing you and your church
could do that would demonstrate the character and love
of Jesus? What could you do that would cause people
to *give glory to your Father in heaven* (Matt. 5:16)?

14. When you consider these questions, what gives you
hope?

15. How could you and your church learn more dependence on the Holy Spirit?

Plan for Action – Part 3

The Love-Truth Matrix

One of the hardest things for us to do as believers is to hold the biblical tension between truth and love. We want to be like Jesus and not skimp on either! As we move closer to the margins, we will find ourselves in more challenging situations where biblical truth must be spoken boldly. At the same time, the world is looking for proof that we are intolerant, hypocrites, and full of hate. Truth must be spoken boldly, but love must also be expressed or the truth will never be heard. The following matrix may help to hold the tension.

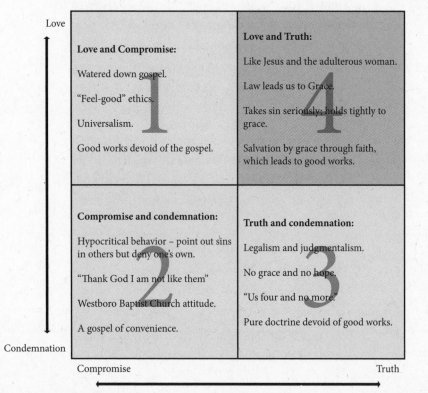

Love

Love and Compromise:

Watered down gospel.

"Feel-good" ethics.

Universalism.

Good works devoid of the gospel.

Love and Truth:

Like Jesus and the adulterous woman.

Law leads us to Grace.

Takes sin seriously; holds tightly to grace.

Salvation by grace through faith, which leads to good works.

Compromise and condemnation:

Hypocritical behavior – point out sins in others but deny one's own.

"Thank God I am not like them"

Westboro Baptist Church attitude.

A gospel of convenience.

Truth and condemnation:

Legalism and judgmentalism.

No grace and no hope.

"Us four and no more."

Pure doctrine devoid of good works.

Condemnation

Compromise   Truth

Working from this matrix, develop a personal plan of action and a church plan of action.

Personal:

1. In what quadrant do you usually find yourself on a daily basis? Which quadrant needs some attention?

2. What beliefs, attitudes, and actions do you need to address in order to move closer to the Love and Truth quadrant? Make this a matter of prayer. Search the Scriptures. Let the Holy Spirit specifically point out what you need to change. He will!

3. Draw out a blank matrix. In the Love and Truth quadrant write down specific action steps the Holy Spirit has shown you. Be specific, especially as it relates to relationships with people – family, neighbors, friends, co-workers, people you don't like!

4. In the other three quadrants, write down specifics the Spirit has shown you that need to be corrected or changed.

5. When you encounter people who radically disagree with you on biblical truth, how can you stay in the Love-Truth quadrant? How do you respond to harsh disagreements, ridicule, unfair accusations, and being ostracized?

6. What are some specific ways you can boldly proclaim truth full of Christ-like love?

Church:

1. In what quadrant does your church usually find itself? What would the people in your community say? What

is your church's reputation? Which quadrant needs some attention?

2. What corporate beliefs, attitudes, and actions does your church need to address in order to move closer to the Love and Truth quadrant? Could it be traditionalism? Being in love with the latest fad? Overt or hidden racism? Some other kind of prejudice? Division in the body? Hostility towards outsiders? A lack of good works? A lack of biblical preaching and teaching? Make this a matter of prayer. Search the Scriptures. Let the Holy Spirit specifically point out what you need to change. He will!

3. Draw out a blank matrix. In the Love and Truth quadrant write down specific action steps the Holy Spirit has shown you that your church can take. Be specific, especially as it relates to relationships with people: the church body, the community, the lost, those antagonistic to the gospel, the people you would rather not come to your church!

4. In the other three quadrants, write down specifics the Spirit has shown you that need to be corrected or changed.

5. When biblical truth is challenged in your church, how can you stay in the Love-Truth quadrant? How do you respond to harsh disagreements, ridicule, unfair accusations, and being ostracized?

6. What are some specific ways your church can boldly proclaim truth full of Christ-like truth?

This return to the margins is not a new status. It has been the predominant and most beneficial status of biblical Christianity in history and currently throughout the world. The margins of society have historically been where the church has lived most fruitfully and spiritual pruning takes place. This is where spiritual awakenings and church revivals often begin. The margins, although frightening in their implications, are exciting because of the new opportunities they present for theology, mission, and ministry.

Whether or not my analysis is close to accurate, we must remember that God is sovereign, and he is on a mission. We are his instruments in that mission to redeem all of creation, and he will not fail.

About the Author

Terry Coy, Ph.D. in theology, has served in missions and church planting since 1992. He has been married to Sandy for over forty years, and they love nothing more than spending time with their four wonderful grandchildren. They all live in the Fort Worth, Texas, area. Terry is also the author of *Facing the Change: Challenges and Opportunities for an American Missiology.*

Connect with Terry:

terryfcoy@gmail.com

Help us help others in our "Make it Public" campaign. If this book helped you and your church, please write a review on Amazon saying what helped most and how it impacts your church.

amazon.com

Also by the Author

The United States is a mission field. The inevitable decline of Christianity as a civil religion and rapid cultural, demographic, and economic change create both serious challenges and hopeful opportunities for the evangelical church in America. In *Facing the Change*, Terry Coy challenges the church to tackle Christological confusion, thoughtfully reconsider the character of American society, and advance boldly and humbly in effectively taking the gospel to a diverse nation. Biblically sound, culturally insightful, and practically challenging, this book is for that thoughtful person trying to get a handle on the meaning of changes in American life and how the church should respond.

Download a free study guide at:
http://sbtexas.com/resources/facing-the-change-study-guide/98/

Available on Amazon.com:

jubilee
B I B L E   2000

*Hear what God is
saying through this
original translation*

ANEKO Press